Colin Alves

The Christian in Education

SCM PRESS LTD

The quotations from *Half our Future* and
Children and their Primary Schools are made by
permission of the Controller of Her Majesty's
Stationery Office; and those from *The Fourth R*
by permission of SPCK and the National Society.

334 00188 9

First published 1972
by SCM Press Ltd
56 Bloomsbury Street London

© *SCM Press Ltd 1972*

Printed in Great Britain by
Richard Clay (The Chaucer Press) Ltd
Bungay, Suffolk

scm centrebooks · christian casebooks

already published
Managing the Church/*W. E. Beveridge*
The Casework Ministry/*Joan B. Miller*
Case Studies in Unity/*R. M. C. Jeffery*
The Christian in Education/*Colin Alves*

in preparation
An Eye for an Ear/*Trevor Beeson*
Solitary Refinement/*Sister Madeleine OSA*

Contents

Contents

Foreword

I have written this book with two kinds of reader in mind. In the first place, it is obvious that there are many people who are puzzled and perhaps concerned by recent developments in education in this country, and particularly by the changes occurring in religious education (or RE, as it is called for short). I have tried to explain exactly what lies behind these changes, and to examine how far someone with a Christian commitment can greet these changes with equanimity.

But I have also had another reader in mind; the person who is already committed to the new educational lines of development and at the same time feels that no Christian comment on (let alone presence within) the educational scene today can be any longer relevant. My hope is that such a person will be persuaded that Christianity is not the sworn enemy he may have believed it to be, and yet at the same time come to recognize that there may be some valid correctives to his position that Christian comment can offer.

I would like to take this opportunity of expressing my thanks to all my colleagues, fellow committee members and fellow commissioners from whom I have learnt so much over this past exciting decade of change and development. My thanks must also go to my friends at the SCM Press who have been so tolerant and encouraging during the writing of this book. And grateful thanks go too to my family for bearing with all the disruption to normal life that an excessively imminent deadline brings with it.

1 By Way of Clarification

'The Christian in . . .' was at one time almost as popular a title-formula as 'The Church and . . .' or (more recently) 'The Theology of . . .'. Frequency of use, however, does not necessarily indicate clarity of meaning. All three of these terms are open to a wide variety of definition, and have also been subjected to a wide variety of use, and misuse. Clarification is therefore called for when someone chooses *The Christian in Education* as the title of a book. Who exactly is being referred to as 'the Christian'?

In an earlier book in the centrebook series John Bowden set out to answer the question 'Who is a Christian?' His answer was not as clear cut as some might have anticipated. He recognizes that many people would want to answer the question 'in quite a specific way, in terms of definite actions, definite commitments', but he himself does not 'believe that there are any such definite answers to be had', nor does he 'think that there is any point in trying to draw distinctions between Christians and non-Christians for most practical purposes' (pp. 11f.). Yet there *is* a distinction, an absolutely fundamental one, as he indicates in his final chapter.

Are Christians no more than men of good will? The question has been raised acutely by the new emphasis on social, international and racial concern within Christianity coupled with the public uncertainty about God and the possibility of religious belief. . . . If what I have been trying to say is true, then being a Christian will not necessarily show obviously on the outside. . . . The kind of life to which Christianity points is not always easily identifiable; the label does not always guarantee

9

the product, nor does the product always bear the label. . . . Where the difference surely comes, however, is in what might best be called the realm of 'self-understanding'. It comes in what Christians understand themselves to be, the interpretation they put on the world, the perspective they bring to it (pp. 115f.).

He illustrates this point with a parable borrowed from John Hick.

> Two men are travelling together along a road. One of them believes that it leads to the Celestial City, the other that it leads nowhere; but since this is the only road there is, both must travel along it. Neither has been this way before; therefore neither is able to say what they will find around each corner. During their journey they meet with moments of refreshment and delight, and with moments of hardship and danger. All the time one of them thinks of his journey as a pilgrimage to the Celestial City. He interprets the pleasant parts as encouragements and the obstacles as trials of his purpose and lessons in endurance, prepared by the king of that city and designed to make of him a worthy citizen of the place when at last he arrives. The other, however, believes none of this, and sees their journey as an unavoidable and aimless ramble. Since he has no choice in the matter, he enjoys the good and endures the bad. For him there is no Celestial City to be reached, no all-encompassing purpose ordaining their journey; there is only the road itself and the luck of the road in good weather and in bad.[1]

It is important (both for an understanding of what 'being a Christian' means, and for following the argument in later stages of this book) to recognize that *neither* of the travellers in Hick's parable claims to be 'able to say what they will find'. The believer does not base his interpretation of the journey on any assertion that he has definite knowledge which is hidden from his companion. His enjoyment, his assurance, his hope are not built on proven and provable facts, but on faith, on trustful belief. In this respect he would be no different from any other optimistic traveller on the road. The astrologer whose personal horoscope for the journey is a propitious one, the old-style liberal evolutionist striding joyfully towards 'tomorrow's world', the Marxist who feels his steps are guided and empowered by the inexorable drive of the dialectic – all these are one with the Christian, in that their various sustaining beliefs are equally *beliefs*, are 'interpretations' of the journey upon which they find themselves embarked.

But there are, of course, differences between these assorted beliefs, not only in content but, more significantly, in their place of grounding. By acknowledging that the various travellers are all travelling in faith rather than in knowledge, one is not asserting that for each traveller it is simply a question of personal choice as to which belief he holds to. Each belief will be grounded in certain phenomena, certain events which have struck the believer as being of especial significance. He has not chosen his belief, he has been captured by it. It is here that we can see the essential characteristic of the Christian, that which distinguishes him in the last resort from those other travellers with whom he has so much in common. The Christian (to adapt a phrase of van Buren's)[2] is one who is 'struck by the biblical story, having always to reckon with this story, and so having continually to revise the way he sees things in the light of how he reads that story'.

The consciousness of having been challenged along these lines may well lead the Christian into actions and activities which are indistinguishable from those of his non-Christian colleagues; it may lead different Christians into widely differing patterns of behaviour and belief. But nevertheless within this Venn diagram, this pattern of overlapping and subdivided sets, there remains a 'Christian constant', a feature which marks Christians out as distinguishable from other people, at the same time binding them together into a single unit despite their manifold internal differences. This constant feature is the fact that each Christian will recognize that, in some way, 'he has been struck by the biblical story'.

If this, then, is what we are to understand by 'the Christian', who is 'the Christian in education' about whom (or

11

for whom) this book is apparently being written? Obviously the category is not to be confined to that small band of people whose service towards their local church community is seen in terms of teaching within it, whether in Sunday school, Bible class, adult group or even in the church day school (though the future of this church-centred educational activity will be examined in a later chapter). Nor, certainly, is the category to be confined to those members of the teaching profession, whether responsible for religious education or not, who 'have accepted Jesus as their Lord and Saviour' and whose whole life is committed to a working out of what they see as 'His Will', whether this be in their own lives or in the lives of others over whom they are enabled to exert any degree of influence. On the other hand, the category is not to be drawn so widely that it will include 'anyone teaching in the western, non-communist world'. As we shall see, many of the values and assumptions underlying western educational thinking could well be claimed as 'Christian values and assumptions', but again this is not to say that the Christian in education has nothing distinctive, or critical, to say about current educational structures in our western society, nor that he has no problems of conscience about participating in some of the practices being encouraged by the exponents of educational innovation (or reaction).

NOTES

1. John Hick, *Philosophy of Religion*, Prentice-Hall 1963, p. 101.
2. In Royal Institute of Philosophy Lectures, Vol. 2, *Talk of God*, Macmillan 1969, p. 53. (The original phrase occurs in van Buren's definition of a *theologian*.)

2 The Educational Scene

It would be foolish in a book of this size to attempt to describe the current educational scene in all its complexity. When the educational shelves contain books whose titles range from *Teaching as a Subversive Activity* to *Moving Progressively Backwards* (alias *Black Paper No. 2:3*), then it is obvious that cohesion of thought and consistency of policy is far from having been achieved. Nevertheless there is a discernible area of opinion and practice which merits the description 'the general current view' inasmuch as it represents what many teachers actually do think and do, and what many others at least feel they *ought* to be thinking and doing.

One can best familiarize oneself with this representative area by reading some of the official reports on various aspects of education published over the past decade. The two basic documents for this exercise are obviously *Half our Future* (HMSO 1963) and *Children and their Primary Schools* (HMSO 1967). Both these volumes are subtitled 'A report of the Central Advisory Council for Education (England)', which is an indication that both are the products of the same official machinery being set in motion, but it should be made absolutely clear that the two reports, despite their common ground, were *not* written by the same group of people. The Council is not a permanent body; it is specifically convened for each task remitted to it and it was in fact almost completely remanned in August 1963, as soon as it had (under the chairmanship of Sir John Newsom) completed its task of 'advising the Minister on the education of pupils aged 13 to

13

16 of average and less than average ability'. The only member held over from that previous operation was Sir John himself, who now became deputy chairman. The new chairman was Lady Plowden and it is therefore her name which is frequently given to the Council's report on its new task of 'considering the whole subject of primary education and the transition to secondary education'.

What view of education comes from these two related yet quite independent reports? The Newsom Report devoted an early chapter to 'Objectives' in which the following opinions are set forth:

> Most teachers and parents would agree with us about general objectives. Skills, qualities of character, knowledge, physical well-being, are all to be desired. Boys and girls need to be helped to develop certain skills of communication in speech and in writing, in reading with understanding, and in calculations involving numbers and measurement: these skills are basic, in that they are tools to other learning and without some mastery of them the pupils will be cut off from whole areas of human thought and experience. But they do not by themselves represent an adequate minimum education at which to aim. All boys and girls need to develop, as well as skills, capacities for thought, judgment, enjoyment, curiosity. They need to develop a sense of responsibility for their work and towards other people, and begin to arrive at some code of moral and social behaviour which is self-imposed. It is important that they should have some understanding of the physical world and of the human society in which they are growing up. How are the schools to set about meeting these deeper educational needs? When parents ask their children what they do at school, the answers tend to be about particular lessons and subjects – arithmetic, woodwork, geography. That is understandable, because that is how the experience of each day is made up. Sometimes it may seem as if that is all school is about, especially to the more dissatisfied customers, who go on to ask 'What's the use?' But it is not the whole of what school really is about. The separate lessons and subjects are single pieces of a mosaic; and what matters most is not the numbers and colours of the separate pieces, but what pattern they make

14

when put together. Some of the most urgent questions which all secondary schools are having to ask themselves just now are about the total patterns of the curriculum, for all their pupils. . . . How is it possible to devise a content of education which exercises their minds and emotions and feeds their imagination? What kinds of experiences will help them to develop their full capacities for thought and taste and feeling? Without some satisfactory answers, both the individual and society remain that much the more impoverished (§ 76, 77, 83).

One notes at once that the major justification for setting objectives along these lines is seen to reside in 'the needs of the pupils'. This is, however, a phrase which has come under considerable critical examination among recent educational writers, who argue that unless the 'needs' can be classified as being fundamentally biological in character, then they offer no real basis of justification for educational practices. Upon what grounds, for example, can one claim that 'all boys and girls need to develop a capacity for enjoyment'? Even if it were shown that mental health (i.e. those mental states which fall within the range of 'normality') is dependent among other things upon a capacity for enjoyment, one would then have to postulate that the establishment of mental health was one objective of education before one could justify certain educational practices by talking about the child's 'need' to develop such a capacity.

Sir John's committee members, however, were not exclusively drawn from the ranks of the new breed of educational philosopher, and so no carefully worded attempt was made to define the really basic objectives of the educational enterprise. But this does not mean to say that no such objectives were present in the minds of the committee. Two, at least, are implied in the passage quoted above, in the final sentence of the passage – namely, the enrichment of the individual and the enrichment of society. (Let us leave for the moment the chicken and egg question implied in the parallelism of this phrase.)

Lady Plowden's committee were more overtly conscious

of the educational philosophers' possible contribution to a statement of objectives (or *aims* of education, as they chose to call them):

It is difficult to reach agreement on the aims of primary education if anything but the broadest terms are used, but formulations of that kind are little more than platitudes. We invited the help of a number of distinguished educationists and professors of educational philosophy, and enjoyed a lengthy and interesting discussion with them. They all confirmed the view that general statements of aims were of limited value, and that a pragmatic approach to the purposes of education was more likely to be fruitful (§ 501).

One such pragmatic approach the committee recognized was to look at what society seemed to be expecting of the schools; for example:

American schools have had, as an avowed purpose, the Americanization of children from different cultures, races and climates. Russian education is strictly geared to particular political and social beliefs (§ 493).

Another pragmatic approach actually used by the committee was to ask the teachers what *they* felt they were aiming at in their work. The teachers consulted

laid emphasis upon the all round development of the individual and upon the acquisition of the basic skills necessary in contemporary society. Many added a third aim, that of the religious and moral development of the child and some a fourth, that of children's physical development and acquisition of motor skills. Phrases such as 'whole personality', 'happy atmosphere', 'full and satisfying life', 'full development of powers', 'satisfaction of curiosity', 'confidence', 'perseverance' and 'alertness' occurred again and again. . . . One of our witnesses gave this list: 'physical health, intellectual development, emotional and moral health, aesthetic awareness, a valid perspective, practical skills, social skills, personal fulfilment', and so on, with each main heading divided into appropriate sub-headings (§ 497, 502).

As a result of all their enquiries and deliberations the members of the Plowden Committee eventually came to the conclusion that

the trend of primary school practices and outlook corresponds to a recognizable philosophy of education, and to a view of society, which may be summarized as follows. A school is not merely a teaching shop, it must transmit values and attitudes. It is a community in which children learn to live first and foremost as children and not as future adults. In family life children learn to live with people of all ages. The school sets out deliberately to devise the right environment for children, to allow them to be themselves and to develop in the way and at the pace appropriate to them. It tries to equalize opportunities and to compensate for handicaps. It lays special stress on individual discovery, on first hand experience and on opportunities for creative work. It insists that knowledge does not fall into neatly separate compartments and that work and play are not opposite but complementary. A child brought up in such an atmosphere at all stages of his education has some hope of becoming a balanced and mature adult and of being able to live in, to contribute to, and to look critically at, the society of which he forms a part (§ 504f.).

Yet this was not their last word on the subject. In the final paragraph of this chapter on 'Aims' one finds once again the case being rested on the basis of 'the interests of the children':

Those interests are complex. Children need to be themselves, to live with other children and with grown ups, to learn from their environment, to enjoy the present, to get ready for the future, to create and to love, to learn to face adversity, to behave responsibly, in a word, to be human beings (§ 507).

It will be noticed that this list of needs does not include the word 'knowledge' (or 'know'), nor has the word appeared in any of the other passages so far quoted (apart from the statement that 'knowledge does not fall into neatly separate compartments'). In fairness to the Plowden Committee, they did anticipate in their argument that they might be accused of neglecting 'knowledge' as such. Their critics, they expected, would assume that 'under the modern regime ... the older virtues, as they are usually called, of neatness, accuracy, care and perseverance, and the sheer knowledge which is an essential of being educated, will decline'. The committee believed that their critics were wrong in assuming that these 'virtues' would decline, and in fact agreed with them about the importance of such matters. 'These are genuine virtues and an education which does not foster them is faulty. ... Children need them and need knowledge, if they are to gain satisfaction from their education.' (§ 506f.)

Nevertheless, despite this attempt to identify common ground, the committee were definitely repudiating one view of education and advocating another, quite distinct, view. It was not an accident that the chapter on 'The Aims of Primary Education' was immediately followed by one called 'Children Learning in School'. There is no chapter called 'Teaching Today', or anything similar. The committee had, in fact, rejected the old picture of the teacher as somebody who has equipped himself with an extensive body of useful knowledge in order to impart it in ordered fashion to those who are put in his charge. Gone was the old metaphor of the child as a *tabula rasa*, waiting eagerly and expectantly for whatever the teacher might inscribe upon his receptive surface, (or, to update the metaphor, the child as a newly built computer, all ready for programming). Gone too was the metaphor of the child as an empty vessel, needing to be filled with a whole variety of objects drawn from the teacher's capacious store. Gone, in fact, was any and every metaphor which depicted the child as passive, merely being the recipient in a process of transmission of knowledge (whether knowledge of facts or knowledge of skills).

In place of such metaphors the Plowden Report sought to establish ones which portray the child as active, and point to learning rather than teaching as the characteristic activity to be found in a school. Two short extracts carry this message with ringing clarity:

'The child is the agent in his own learning' (§ 529).

18

'Learning takes place through a continuous process of inter-action between the learner and his environment' (§ 521).

The teacher's essential function therefore is not the purvey-ing of facts, or the developing of skills; it is the organizing of the environment in such a way as to enable the pupils to learn most effectively. However knowledgeable the teacher may in fact be, it is from their environment that his pupils learn, not from him (except in so far as he is inevitably part of that environment).

This view of the teacher's role demands that the process of education is seen as a wide open process, not confined by the limits of the teacher's actual knowledge, nor geared to the production of an exact replica of the teacher's own outlook on life in the minds of his pupils.

The sort of metaphor which most aptly conveys this view of the educational process is one which involves *growth*. John Dewey, the American educationist and philosopher, in fact went so far as to apply the metaphor in a starkly literal sense by claiming that 'education *is* growth', but let us for our present purposes stick with the idea as a metaphor. The teacher may then be seen as a gardener whose job it is to feed and water his plants. The *raison d'être* of the whole process is the fostering of growth within the plant, and with-out the prior operation of that growth the gardener's labours are in vain. Growth *precedes* the gardener's ministrations; he was not the originator of the process, he merely en-countered it and tried to help it on its way.

Now I have been deliberately using the gardening meta-phor because 'educational growth' is often talked of as if it were exactly parallel with 'plant growth'. This identification in fact leads to a number of ambiguities. For example, it will be noted that I have said nothing so far about those fairly frequent duties of real (as opposed to metaphorical) garden-ers, such as weeding, pruning, tying in, training, layering, grafting, hybridizing – in other words all those activities which are intended to modify growth, or to redirect growth, rather than simply to promote free growth.

There are not many educational writers today (though there are indeed *some*) who would say with Rousseau 'Let us lay it down as an incontrovertible rule that the first impulses of nature are always right; there is no original sin in the human heart.'[1] On this basis, of course, opportunity for free growth would be all that is required for 'education' to take place, and the teacher's task would presumably be simply to protect the growing subject from such influences as might cause his growth to become stunted. Given such protection, and therefore given real freedom to grow, the goal of growth would be inevitably obtained, the fully developed blossom would burst forth from its bud to the delight of all who viewed it. Certainly there will be in the garden a few plants whose blossoms are in some way deformed, have remained only half open, have prematurely lost their petals, or have even died outright before flowering, but the Rousseauist would hasten to explain all these phenomena in terms of pests, adverse weather conditions, environmentally acquired diseases and so on. The inner fount of growth, on this view, is in its essence unsullied.

However, as I said before, not many educationists still fully maintain Rousseau's gloriously optimistic account of the nature of 'growth' in the human being. Even if we persist with the gardening metaphor we have to accept that plant growth can from its very beginnings be malfunctioning and distorted, sickly and unfruitful. It can also very rapidly become cankerous or a source of infection for other plants growing near by. The gardener's job, then, calls for far more than simple 'tending'. He has standards of 'healthy growth' which he will wish to promote and achieve.

But another, more fundamental, weakness of the gardening metaphor reveals itself at this point, for the truth is that the gardener is limited (unless he quite deliberately 'tampers' with his plants) by the biological processes operating within each specimen. A rosebush can do no other than produce a rose; an onion seed will produce an onion, not a daffodil, not even a leek. But the human child is not confined in this way. There may well be a biological limitation on his bio-logical growth (pigmentation, facial features, etc.) but his *educational* growth is open to a wide variety of outcomes – not a limitless variety, admittedly, but nevertheless a variety of sufficient range to make educational growth totally distinct in quality from biological growth.

This point is well made in R. F. Dearden's *The Philosophy of Primary Education*, in the chapter in which he examines 'growth' as a possible 'aim' of education. On the whole he finds 'growth' to be a confusing concept to use in this way and suggests that it has outlived its usefulness. However, to say this does imply that it has had its uses in the past, and towards the end of his argument Dearden asks 'Is there anything of ethical value embedded in the growth ideology which, when extracted, is seen to be acceptable? Our own suggestion is that there certainly is.' He suggests in fact that an ideal, a basic human ideal, is hidden within the whole metaphorical system which has been built around (one hardly dare say 'has sprung up around') the idea of growth as an educational aim. The exact definition of this ideal we will return to a little later. The immediate purpose of this excursion into Dearden's arguments is to note how he explains the tremendous popularity, among liberal educationists, of the growth ideology. He suggests that in searching for the ideal they found the ideology and became diverted by it from the real goal of their endeavour.

> In conclusion it might be worth indicating how the valuable core of the growth ideology that has been extracted here should so readily have been confused with quasi-biological notions of growth, and of the unfolding and flowering of inner potentialities. There are two main points of analogy between the human ideal and the natural process which invite the conflation. First, the ideal is opposed to any kind of authoritarian dictation or imposition, whether by parties, priests or public pressures. Analogously, growth is from within and is to be contrasted with moulding from without.
>
> Secondly, the ideal and 'growth' both involve continuity

and movement in a definite direction, though in one case there
is self-direction and in the other only a biological process.[2]

Education, then, (even if one rejects the actual metaphor of
growth, particularly with all its horticultural ramifications)
is still seen as something dynamic, as opposed to the static,
passive metaphors of children as pages to be written upon or
buckets to be filled. 'Movement in a definite direction' is
involved. But in what direction? In the direction of the
acquisition of certain knowledge? Have we come subtly
round to a position we appeared to abandon with the rejection of the static metaphors? Far from it. Even though the
word 'understanding' is frequently employed in his arguments, Dearden's own position could hardly be called
knowledge-centred, or subject-centred, certainly not in the
traditional sense of these terms. In fact he is *less* bound by
these traditional concerns than is the Plowden Report. We
have already noted that the Report warns us 'that knowledge
does not fall into neatly separate compartments' (§ 505);
Dearden comments on this, 'the Report itself then proceeds
to a discussion of the curriculum which is divided into eleven
separate and conventional subject compartments' (§ 555ff.).
We have also already noted how anxious the Committee
were to repudiate any suggestion that they 'wished to under-
value knowledge and facts' (§ 529) and went as far as to
speak of 'the sheer knowledge which is an essential of being
educated' (§ 506).

But *what* knowledge and *which* facts did they see as valu-
able, as essential? The answer to this question does not
emerge easily and clearly, even from the long chapter on
'Aspects of the Curriculum' which Dearden pokes fun at.
One suspects that, despite their protestations, the Committee
did not value 'knowledge and facts' in the way that many of
their critics did, namely as ends in themselves. For them
knowledge was important as a means, or rather as raw
material upon which other processes could then get to work,
the processes and not the raw material being what was of real
value. Certainly this is the view held by John Holt, whose

book *How Children Fail* is referred to in a footnote to paragraph 531 of the Report.

In his blistering summary of 'how *schools* fail' Holt writes:

> Behind much of what we do in school lie some ideas that could be expressed roughly as follows: (1) Of the vast body of human knowledge there are certain bits and pieces that can be called essential, that everyone should know; (2) the extent to which a person can be considered educated, qualified to live intelligently in today's world and be a useful member of society, depends on the amount of this essential knowledge that he carries about with him; (3) it is the duty of the schools, therefore, to get as much of this essential knowledge as possible into the minds of the children.
>
> These ideas are absurd and harmful nonsense. We don't and can't agree on what knowledge is essential. Moreover, we cannot possibly judge what knowledge will be most needed forty, or twenty, or even ten years from now. Since we can't know what knowledge will be most needed in the future, it is senseless to try to teach it in advance. Instead we should try to turn out people who love learning so much and learn so well that they will be able to learn whatever needs to be learned.
>
> A child who is learning naturally, following his curiosity where it leads him, adding to his mental model of reality whatever he needs and can find a place for, and rejecting without fear or guilt what he does not need, is growing – in knowledge, in the love of learning, and in the ability to learn. All his life he will go on learning. Every experience will make his mental model of reality more complete and more true to life, and thus make him more able to deal realistically, imaginatively, and constructively with whatever new experience life throws his way. . . . For the test of true intelligence is not how much we know how to do, but how we behave when we don't know what to do.[3]

Clearly for Holt the acquisition of *any* knowledge, the investigation of *any* facts will serve his purpose. He says so in so many words: 'The school should be a great smörgåsbrod of intellectual, artistic, creative and athletic activities, from which each child could take whatever he wanted.

Choosing what he wants to learn and what he does not is something he must do for himself. . . . For when it is *real* learning one piece of learning is as good as another.'[4]

This last phrase will of course cause paroxysms of mirth or anger to descend upon anyone who is even vaguely familiar with the work of Professor Hirst and those associated with him.[5] Hirst has argued that 'learning' is a word which covers a wide variety of different processes, and cannot possibly be used in the totally non-specific way that Holt has tried to do here. Even Holt himself seems to recognize that all acts of learning are *not* indiscriminately interchangeable when he suggests that the smörgåsbrod should consist of 'intellectual, artistic, creative and athletic activities', and presumably even he would not claim that a child who has learnt to play the clarinet would have benefited himself in the long run in exactly the same way as if he had learnt to do quadratic equations.

Nevertheless Holt does seem to lump all 'intellectual' activity together as if all processes of intellectual learning were one and the same, maths (for example) being differentiated from history simply by virtue of its field of subject matter. What Hirst has reminded us is that not only are there different *fields* of knowledge, but there are quite distinct *forms* of understanding. These *forms* can be distinguished on a number of grounds, but the most clear-cut seems to be the method of validation used by each form. Thus the scientific form of understanding depends upon observation and experiment to validate its assumptions; the mathematical/logical form depends upon the operation of tightly reasoned argument within a given system of axioms; the historical form validates its assertions about past events (and their present consequences) by a process having more in common with what occurs in a court of law than the processes of the scientific experimenter; the ethical form depends even more heavily on 'judgment', though it is not entirely divorced from empirical considerations (the consequences of actions have to be calculated before their appro-

24

priateness can be decided upon); the aesthetic form of understanding demands a considerable measure of subjective identification with the activity or object of which understanding is being sought, as well as sufficient familiarity with the general field for some standard of comparison to be objectively applied. (The difficulties of establishing 'validity' for aesthetic understanding are notorious. Can one ever be sure that one understands someone else's music or painting 'rightly', or that a composer or painter knows when he is producing 'valid' work? Yet Hirst's point is clearly illustrated by these difficulties inasmuch as it would obviously be absurd to try and answer these questions by turning them into ones which could be answered purely in scientific, mathematical, historical or ethical terms.)

As well as these distinct forms of understanding, Hirst has identified within the complex processes of learning the acquisition of 'practical skills'. These include a whole variety of physical skills, such as learning to throw a ball, to knock in a nail, to draw a straight line, as well as the basic 'intellectual' skills of reading, counting and communicating intelligibly.

In the light of such an analysis of the different types of learning of which the human organism is capable, it is indeed a dramatic oversimplification to say that 'one piece of learning is as good as another'. And yet one can appreciate what Holt is pleading for. Even though Dearden follows Hirst closely and would therefore totally reject Holt's claim that a healthy educational diet can only be provided by a totally free self-service running buffet, nevertheless he would endorse his assertion that 'the ability to learn' must take priority over 'the acquisition of knowledge'. Of course Dearden will rightly have nothing of the idea that 'the ability to learn' means no more than the acquisition of a 'universal information-getting skill' which 'roughly comprises a knowledge of the usefulness of reference books and of their classification, together with a certain facility in scanning indexes and tables of contents'.[6] What Holt would call 'intelligence' (the ability to cope with new experience) has a lot in common with what

25

Dearden calls 'understanding'. Having understanding (of, and within, each respective 'form') involves the ability to recognize the underlying structures of a situation, and so to select the appropriate procedures for investigating or responding to it. This is obviously not the same as knowing certain facts about it; it may be a totally new situation. Understanding, therefore, is much more fundamental, much more widely applicable than knowledge. It also gives a man much more freedom than factual knowledge can, both freedom of useful response in new situations and also freedom from imposed patterns of response in familiar situations. This is not irrelevant to the fact that 'autonomy' is such an important word in Dearden's argument. Reference was made earlier in this chapter to the 'ideal' which he had identified as determining the aim of liberal educationists. This ideal he defines as 'a personal autonomy based on reason', and goes on to comment:

> There are two aspects to such an autonomy, the first of which is negative. This is independence of authorities, both of those who would dictate or prescribe what I am to believe and of those who would arbitrarily direct me in what I am to do. The complementary positive aspect is, first, that of testing the truth of things for myself, whether by experience or by a critical estimate of the testimony of others, and, secondly, that of deliberating, forming intentions and choosing what I shall do according to a scale of values which I can myself appreciate. Both understanding and choice, or thought and action, are therefore to be independent of authority and based instead on reason. This is the ideal.

Dearden sums up his comments by saying that 'the central values' of the educational ideal he is advocating are:

> Independence, reason,
> Integrity, truth,
> Freedom of individual choice and judgment concerning what is worthwhile,
> Responsibility and fairness.[7]

26

This emphasis on autonomy, independence, freedom of individual choice, which is so central to Dearden's 'ideal' and which was equally central (through the metaphors of 'growth') to the Plowden Report, has been the most characteristic feature of educational thinking over the past few years. It reached its clearest expression (and, in the eyes of some, its final absurdity) in the concept of 'teacher neutrality' advocated by Lawrence Stenhouse in connection with the Schools Council Integrated Humanities scheme.[8]

The method of operation employed by this scheme was to take some controversial area from human life, like war or sexual mores, and to provide for the 14–15 year olds (for whom the scheme was devised) a whole pack of material representing diverse points of view. The teacher's task was to introduce the pupils to the material, and to ensure that the questions they asked of the material were logically appropriate ones. Any conclusions, therefore, which were reached by the pupils would be their *own* conclusions, influenced solely by the facts of the case and the validity of the opinions examined. The teacher was to remain entirely neutral and was not to allow his viewpoint on the issue to become apparent. The reason for this was that his position within the group was felt to carry such authority that, were he to disclose his own views, the pupils would all tend either to agree with them or to disagree with them merely on the grounds that 'teacher says so'; and this would obviously not be conducive to rational autonomy of thought.

A fairly similar argument lies behind the position adopted by John Wilson with regard to Moral Education.[9] For Wilson the processes of moral education should not be those which enable the teacher to develop within the pupils patterns of moral behaviour which reflect his own patterns (or those of the particular society he represents); they should be those which promote in the pupils the ability to make moral judgments for themselves, to bring rational thought to bear on moral dilemmas. The teacher should therefore take care to present even conventional views (his own or anyone else's)

27

as material for *study* and not necessarily as patterns for emulation. This, it will be noted, contrasts sharply with the position taken by the Newsom Committee:

> For our part we are agreed that boys and girls should be offered firm guidance on sexual morality based on chastity before marriage and fidelity within it (§ 164).

Another point of difference between the Newsom Report and more recent writing about moral education is that the latter tries to separate morality and religion, so far is as possible, whereas the former was reasonably happy to treat the two as interwoven. Moreover, the whole chapter on spiritual and moral development in the former appears to have been written from a specifically Christian point of view. This is by no means the case with much of more recent comment on the treatment of moral and similarly controversial issues in the classroom. Does this suggest that the whole movement pressing for teacher neutrality, or at least for pupil autonomy, will inevitably be unacceptable to those who would call themselves Christians?

There are various grounds for thinking that this might indeed be the case. The traditional Christian doctrines of the fall of man, of revelation and of redemption would seem to challenge at its very root the assertion that part of the ideal towards which our educational processes are geared must be 'freedom of individual choice and judgment concerning what is worthwhile'. One of the most respected voices speaking for Christianity in this country in the first half of this century was that of William Temple,[10] and it was Temple who, at the very moment he was repudiating any Barthian overstatement of the position, nevertheless claimed that the fall of man has made revelation an absolute necessity for man if he is to know the truth and perform it.

> We totally misconceive alike the philosophic and the practical problem of evil if we picture it as the winning of control over lawless and therefore evil passions by a righteous but insufficiently powerful reason or spirit. It is the spirit which is

evil. ... Reason itself as it exists in us is vitiated (*Nature, Man and God*, p. 368).

That revelation is altogether other than rational inference from previous experience is vitally important; that only by revelation and by surrender to its spiritual power can man be 'saved' is a profound and irrefragable truth. ... What is quite certain is that the self cannot by any effort of its own lift itself off its own self as centre and resystematize itself about God as its centre. Such radical conversion ... cannot be a process only of enlightenment. Nothing can suffice but a redemptive act. Something impinging on the self from without must deliver it (*ibid.*, pp. 396f.).

When one reads passages like these it would indeed be easy to come away with the impression that the only valid form of education open to the Christian is one which transmits revealed truth and inculcates revealed patterns of behaviour, without which the children must remain in the otherwise irredeemable ignorance of their original sin. Passages such as the following (from Temple's *Christianity and Social Order*) might seem to confirm the impression:

The development of individual gifts under a predominant motive of self-seeking is an injury both to the individual and to society. ... In other words if a man is going to be a knave, it is desirable both for society and for himself that he should also be a fool. To quicken the wits of those who will afterwards use them to prey upon their neighbours is an evident injury to society, but it is a still greater injury to them. ... We are not training children according to their own true nature or in relation to their true environment unless we are training them to trust in God (pp. 67, 69).

Note the use of the word 'training' here. It suggests yet another metaphor to set alongside the empty page, the unprogrammed computer, the empty bucket. It suggests the circus animal, by nature wild or even surly, needing to be subjected to a rigorous (if kindly) programme of training before it is able to share with his trainer in the eventual

29

glories of the big top. Such a metaphor hardly matches up with the ideal of rational autonomy. Does this mean, therefore, that that ideal is not one to which the Christian can subscribe, or was Temple's apparent insistence on 'training' not representative of the Christian position after all?

To begin to answer that question one must recognize that the passage quoted above does not reflect the totality of Temple's views about education. Quite different views emerge alongside this concern for 'training':

> The whole forward movement of our social life turns on the development among the great mass of the people of that kind of education which makes men eager both to think for themselves and to appreciate the truth in any opinion from which they dissent (*Essays in Christian Politics*, p. 76).

There may at first sight seem to be a basic inconsistency between Temple's insistence that it is only by 'surrender to revelation' that a man can be saved and this concern for appreciating truth in opinion different from one's own. But these two positions would only be inconsistent if Temple had taken a strictly verbalist view of revelation, and this was far from the case.

> It is not inappropriate that the term Revelation should be commonly used with a special reference to events – be it a deliverance of a nation from bondage in despite of all calculable probabilities, be it the Incarnation in a human life of that Self-Utterance of God which is the ground of the created universe. But in these events there is no imparting of truth as the intellect apprehends truth. There is event and appreciation; and in the coincidence of these the revelation consists. From all this it follows that there is no such thing as revealed truth. There are truths of revelation, that is to say, propositions which express the results of correct thinking concerning revelation; but they are not themselves directly revealed (*Nature, Man and God*, pp. 312ff.).

Moreover

Revelation given through the reason and conscience of men is usually imperfect. The existence of sin introduces a defect, and it may be a distortion, into all revelation given through the medium of human personality, unless there be found an instance of this which is free from sin (*ibid.*, p. 306).

One can now see why Temple was so concerned to foster the type of education which would result in a growth of tolerance. For him even the possession, in the scriptures, of 'propositions which express the results of correct thinking concerning revelation' could not justify the claim that here was the only source of truth, and an infallible source at that. In matters social and political he rejected all dogmatic partisanship:

> We shall still have our own convictions about what is true and our own judgments about what is expedient ... but in all controversy our aim will be to appreciate and incorporate in our own theory or action all that we can find good or wise in the views of our opponents. We shall strive for the truth as we have seen it, but we shall never suppose that there is no truth but what we have seen (*York enthronement address*).

But his views about revelation took him further than this. Even the area of religious belief had to be one in which tolerance was essential, not because of any wildly relativist principle, but because God's revelation of himself could not of necessity be confined to one propositional system. Temple certainly wanted to defend the uniqueness of Christ, but this did not tie him to any assertion that the Christian church had been granted a monopoly of divine self-revelation. The very least a Christian can, indeed must, do is to respect the beliefs of others, in religion as well as in politics.

> One great gain that the scientific use of the comparative method in religion has brought us is the duty of genuine reverence for other men's beliefs. To reverence them is not at all the same thing as to accept them as necessarily true, but whatever thoughts any human soul is seeking to live by, deserve the reverence of every other human soul (*The Universality of Christ*, p. 22).

But perhaps even more important than Temple's understanding of revelation, and the need for humble tolerance that this view engendered, was his recognition that by virtue of his creation at God's hand each individual person was worthy of total respect and consideration from his fellow creatures.

> The root of democracy is respect for individual personality. At this point democracy closely touches Christianity, which teaches the infinite worth of every individual. By three tests can it be known whether democracy is true to its own root principle: by the depth of its concern for justice to individuals; by the careful regard which it pays to the rights of minorities; by the scrupulous respect which it offers to whatever can present itself in the name of individual conscience. Of these the last is the most vital of all (*Essays in Christian Politics*, pp. 73f., 77).

> A social system which aims at being in accordance with facts will deal with every human being as of unique and irreplaceable value, because he is a child of God (*ibid.*, p. 9).

> If we are going to show a real respect to each individual as a child of God, we must see that from infancy to full maturity every child is set in such a social context as will best develop all the powers which God has given him. To provide such an opportunity, not for a favoured few, but for all children, is an urgent national duty (*Christianity and Social Order*, p. 66).

> The equality that is precious is not equality of powers or gifts, which does not exist; it is an equality of inherent worth and of the right of every individual to be himself (*Christ in His Church*, p. 81).

'The right of every individual to be himself.' This phrase would not be out of place on the lips of the most radical of anti-authoritarian orators. 'Freedom' is of course the most universal of battlecries today, more so even than 'Justice' or 'Brotherhood'. Adolescent rebellion in its contemporary form (as well as its prolongation into middle age in certain manifestations of the 'counter-culture') seems to be based

32

not so much on the feeling that the pattern of life adopted by the parent generation is necessarily a bad pattern, but rather on a feeling of resentment that *any* pattern of life (good or bad) should be imposed upon the rising generations. 'It's *my* life and I can do what I like with it' is the spoken or unspoken assertion lying behind much of the behaviour in the field of sex, drugs and even violence which has captured such constant public attention over the past few years.

As we have already seen, the word 'freedom' and the phrase 'individual development' feature large not only in the underground press but also in contemporary educational writing. We have already met the word 'autonomy' filling a key role. Now it would not be forcing the meaning of 'autonomy' to translate it as 'being a law unto oneself'. Is this really the condition that contemporary education is trying to develop within its pupils? And was Temple aiding and abetting such development when he gave such prominence to 'the right of every individual to be himself'?

Temple's use of this phrase must of course be seen in the context of the whole of his writing. The crucial question is what Temple understood by the words 'being oneself'. In other words, what did he believe to be the true nature of man? Could it be said that someone was 'being himself' if he elected to spend his whole life half-buried in sand inhaling opium, or if he concentrated his whole attention on the problems involved in committing at least one undetected child-murder each week? There are clearly some people who would say 'Yes' to this, who would say that if a person is 'doing his own thing', then he is indeed 'being himself'. One has only to look at the events and attitudes brought to light during the Charles Manson trial to see this belief in full operation. But this was not Temple's understanding of the phrase. In a passage which we will return to later he wrote:

Man is capable of and destined for fellowship with the eternal God. Consequently his choice of ends – his choice between good and evil – not only has consequences for his neighbours or for the society of which he is a member, but has eternal significance for himself and even for God. And this is the basis of his claim to freedom, his claim to be himself, to live his own life and fulfil his own destiny (*The Church Looks Forward*, p. 80).

Freedom to live one's own life is, therefore, in Temple's view, not simply freedom to do what one likes (though it inevitably *involves* that), but freedom to attain to that condition of which every man is capable, fellowship with God. And certain patterns of life will help in the attainment of this condition, whereas others will not. In other words the freedom 'to be oneself', in Christian terms, is a qualified freedom, not an absolute freedom. But it must immediately be emphasized that to talk of a qualified freedom is not to advocate the placing of restrictions upon freedom; it is to indicate that the freedom given to each individual, if it is to be used properly, should be used with certain ends in view rather than others.

This is of course exactly the position adopted by Dearden in his definition of an acceptable educational ideal. The autonomy he advocates is a qualified autonomy, inasmuch as it is *rational* autonomy and is held within a context of 'integrity, truth, responsibility and fairness'. Similarly M. V. C. Jeffreys claims that

a man is free in proportion as his choices contribute to his fuller growth as a rational and responsible person, and that he is unfree in proportion as his choices have the opposite effect of stultifying his faculties or ruining his health. Freedom thus includes self-limitation, or self-discipline.[11]

Jeffreys also talks of 'man's responsibility for making the best of himself', thereby revealing that he too is basing his definitions of freedom (*qualified* freedom) on a particular assumption about the nature of man. The simple truth is that no argument about freedom in education, indeed no argument about freedom in general, can avoid starting out from certain assumptions (which can be no more than assumptions) about the nature of man. The claim that each person ought to be entirely free to 'do his own thing', whatever it may be, assumes it to be quite incontrovertible that man has *no* responsibility for 'making the best of himself'; if he has any responsibility at all, it will merely be to make *something* of himself whereby to assert his independence of the rest of existence.

This very negative view of freedom (and of responsibility, if on this view it exists at all) is not one to which I believe a Christian can subscribe. However much individual Christians may disagree with certain details of Temple's position, I cannot imagine that any would reject his underlying assumption, namely that 'man is capable of and destined for fellowship with the eternal God'. (Radicals and conservatives may argue as to how exactly this phrase is to be unpacked, but both, if they hold any form of Christian allegiance, will surely agree that the phrase does have meaning and significance, or at any rate can perform a significant and valid function.)

But once this basic view of man is assumed, then it follows that man's freedom can only be properly realized in a self-fulfilling way. And it further follows that any educational practice which leads to stultification is open to the charge of blasphemously interfering with the course of man's true destiny. Stultification can occur either as the result of refusing to allow men to exercise their God-given faculty of choice, or equally as the result of allowing them to choose irresponsibly, without self-discipline, without self-understanding. The Christian, then, will be totally opposed to any rigidly structured educational system, in which every pupil follows a curriculum laid down in every detail, allowing no optional, individual variation whatsoever; he will be equally opposed to a Holt-style smörgåsbrod in which choice of activities is left entirely to the individual pupil, resulting in very narrow curricular experience based purely (in most cases) on existing personal interests.

The conviction that every pupil should have some control over his own curriculum and yet at the same time be required to develop (at least to some extent) his interests and potentialities in *each* of the major areas of human activity, is expressed in a number of passages in the Durham Report.[12]

It is a platitude to say that education is concerned with 'the whole man', but it is a platitude that is true and important. It warns us against two dangers. One is that of neglecting the findings of empirical science. If man is not just 'a naked ape' he is at least that. The other is that of taking too limiting a view of human potentialities and one that is too narrowly circumscribed by contemporary fashion (§ 134).

In giving this issue further consideration we recalled that section 7 of the 1944 Education Act contained an introductory statement of general principles, viz:

It shall be the duty of the LEA for every area so far as their powers extend, to contribute towards the spiritual, moral, mental and physical development of the community by securing that efficient education shall be available.

We suggest that any new Education Act should attempt to define more precisely, though only in brief outline, the essential basic components of the education to be given to all pupils at school. The Act might, we think, lay down that *all pupils in county and voluntary schools shall be provided, according to their ages, abilities, and aptitudes, with education in the arts and sciences, in religion and morals, and in physical and practical skills* (§ 574f.).

Dearden too, by virtue of his concern for *rational* autonomy, would have the schools prescribe a broad, common area of activity for all their pupils.

If the school is not to prejudge the choice of the values by which one is to live, this does not mean that it has no role at all in relation to that choice, for rational choice is rich in presuppositions. First, and most importantly, it presupposes that one will indeed choose, and not just be told what to believe and do. To presuppose that is already to take for granted the value of personal autonomy. But the exercise of rational choice also presupposes a well grounded understanding of one's situation in the world. This leads on to the fundamental question: what forms of understanding are basic constitutive elements in rational choice? The answer to this would seem to be as follows: mathematical, scientific, historical, aesthetic and ethical.[13]

(Dearden notes, in a later passage, the additional need to provide for the acquisition of the 'basic skills', and for the physical education of the pupils.)

What these two passages have in common is far more important than the differences between them. They are both based on the conviction that despite the basic principle that each individual must be free to make his own value judgments and consequent decisions, nevertheless (in order to allow this principle to operate conjointly with other basic principles, such as the need for rationality) each individual should be required to undergo educational experience across the full spectrum of basic human activity, however this may be categorized.

I have already referred to this as involving a *qualified* form of freedom, and this phrase brings us back once again to the idea of 'teacher neutrality' mentioned in connection with the names of Lawrence Stenhouse and (to a slightly lesser degree) John Wilson. It would seem that the extreme application of teacher neutrality, wherein the teacher absolutely refuses to express an opinion and acts merely as arbiter between various viewpoints displayed in the material or put forward by the pupils themselves – this form of the doctrine would seem to be based either on the assumption that there are no checks on man's freedom, that man has no responsibility for 'making the best of himself' (except in terms of sheer, intellectualized rationality), or else on the fallacy that one can dispense with assumptions altogether when considering controversial issues.

There is a further fallacy in the extreme form of the doctrine, and one which is not entirely absent from some of its milder forms as well, namely an over-reliance on intellectual argument. Let me make it quite clear that I, as a Christian, have no quarrel with, say, the ideal of rational autonomy, and would have considerable quarrel with any proposed ideal of irrational autonomy. Yet it would seem to me to be a straight, empirically established fact that many basic educational processes start from the impact of person upon person, the whole person upon the whole person, not just mind upon mind. And therefore it would be educationally restrictive, to quite a serious degree, to insist that the teacher should adopt permanently a role in which only his discriminatory faculties and his sense of logical propriety were allowed to operate.

There is, however, a further reservation which the Christian must register when faced with any such demand that the teacher should entirely suppress his own opinions, his own basic assumptions, his own commitments. So much of a teacher's work involves relationships. A good relationship with one's class is a prerequisite of good teaching. A large amount of what children learn has to do with relationships, between individuals, between communities. For a Christian, this area is one of paramount importance, and it is quite impossible to divorce relationship-building from the commitments one holds (or, rather, by which one is held). It is therefore quite impossible for a Christian teacher to forget his Christian commitment, his belief in the implicit value of each individual pupil. It is also impossible for him to subscribe to the view that his only responsibility as a teacher is to help his pupils develop adequate rationality;[14] he is also concerned that they shall develop adequate relationships. At times there arise conflicts between these two concerns, as when for example a pupil persists in misremembering certain facts, and becomes more and more resentful towards the teacher every time he is corrected. Is the establishment of factual accuracy more important than the establishment (or maintenance) of a sound relationship between teacher and pupil? The combination of teacher neutrality with an ideal of rational understanding would seem to give priority to the establishment of factual accuracy. By contrast the teacher whose concerns are coloured by Christ's teaching about the centrality of love might in these circumstances see the force

38

of Dostoevsky's otherwise dangerous assertion, 'If anyone were to prove to me that Christ was outside truth and that truth was really outside Christ, I would still rather remain with Christ than with truth.'[15]

The argument of this chapter may appear to have wandered around, viewing a whole variety of different topics and different positions, but underlying it all has been the concept of individual freedom and the extent to which, if at all, such a concept needs qualifying. Where recent educational writings have emphasized the centrality of personal autonomy as both an ideal and an underlying assumption, then the Christian will heartily endorse this emphasis. He will at the same time affirm that in order to understand the phrase 'being oneself' one has to discover further underlying assumptions about the nature of man. There are in current thinking a number of such assumptions, ranging from radical nihilism to rigid cultural conservatism, from biological determinism to a neo-pelagian do-it-yourself approach to personality development – and many more. The Christian will give a large measure of support to the assertion that personal autonomy should be grounded in rationality, in integrity, in responsible attitudes towards the truth and towards others, but he will want to add two comments: that where concern for intellectual integrity and concern for persons conflict, one should not automatically give priority to intellectual integrity every time; and that 'a responsible attitude' to people is of little use in itself, but needs to move from the conceptual level and find expression in living, growing relationships. (Linus' remark from the world of *Peanuts* is horribly revealing in this respect: 'I love mankind. It's *people* I can't stand.'[16])

We have been concerning ourselves so far with the extent of the Christian's ability to identify himself with some of the theoretical positions being adopted by educationists today. There remains the very practical problem of what happens when ideas and values the Christian teacher would support are noticeably absent from the educational institution or educational system in which he serves. This will indeed occupy our attention in some measure in a later chapter, but first we must pursue the basic theoretical issues into the field where many people (not necessarily correctly) feel the Christian teacher has a particular concern – the field of specifically religious education.

NOTES

1. J. J. Rousseau, *Emile*, Book 2, 1762.
2. R. F. Dearden, *The Philosophy of Primary Education*, Routledge & Kegan Paul 1968, pp. 48f.
3. John Holt, *How Children Fail*, Penguin Books 1969, pp. 171–5, 163.
4. *Ibid.*, pp. 174–6.
5. See e.g. Paul Hirst, 'The Logical and Psychological Aspects of Teaching a Subject', *The Concept of Education*, ed. R. S. Peters, Routledge & Kegan Paul 1967.
6. Dearden, *op. cit.*, p. 62.
7. *ibid.*, pp. 46, 67.
8. See *The Humanities Project: an Introduction*, Heinemann 1970.
9. See John Wilson *et al.*, *Introduction to Moral Education*, Penguin Books 1968.
10. The Publishers and dates of the books from which quotations are taken as illustrations of Temple's thought are as follows:
Christ in His Church, Macmillan & Co. 1924
Christianity and Social Order, Penguin Books 1942
Essays in Christian Politics, Longmans 1927
Nature, Man and God, Macmillan & Co. 1934
The Church Looks Forward, Macmillan & Co. 1944
The Universality of Christ, SCM Press 1921
A useful 'reader' will be found in A. E. Baker, *William Temple and his Message*, Penguin Books 1946.
11. M. V. C. Jeffreys, *Education: its Nature and Purpose*, Allen & Unwin 1971, pp. 29f.
12. Details of the origins and publication of this report will be found in the next chapter.
13. Dearden, *op. cit.*, p. 60.

14. A rather similar position to this view that rationality comes before all else can be found, somewhat unexpectedly, in the Schools Council paper on *Religious Education in Secondary Schools* (see next chapter for details). There it is asserted that 'schools are neither religious nor civic, but academic institutions. So far as teaching and learning are concerned, their primary loyalty is to the onward-going enterprise of scholars in the various fields of disciplined investigation. This is what is meant by academic freedom: the teacher is primarily responsible to the community of scholars rather than to any other social body' (p. 27). Such remarks may well be applicable to universities, but schools surely have wider and more complex responsibilities than this. (Are not parents a 'social body' to whom the schools are in some large measure responsible?) Perhaps the phrase 'so far as teaching and learning are concerned' was intended to be taken in a very strict, classroom-based sense. We return to this general consideration in chapter 4.

15. From a letter to Natalya Fonvisin. Quoted on p. 191 of *Dostoevsky: a Life*, by David Magarshack, Secker & Warburg 1962.

16. © 1959, United Feature Syndicate, Inc. From *Peanuts* by Charles M. Schulz.

41

3　The Christian and Religious Education

The previous chapter opened with a comment about the difficulty of surveying the full complexity of the current educational scene. The situation regarding religious education is hardly less complex. Once again therefore I propose to turn to the official reports as being representative of 'the general current view', though in this instance it will soon become apparent that even the official reports do not all speak with the same voice.

Indeed, the Newsom Report itself seems to a reader today to have been speaking with a somewhat uncertain voice, if not quite a divided one (as the Plowden Report found itself doing four years later). *Half our Future* seems to stand at a watershed: on one side lies the whole tradition of education as a process in which church and state were partners, a tradition stretching back to 1833 and receiving successive reinforcement from the Education Acts of 1870, 1902 and 1944; on the other side lie the 'open fields' of current liberal educational theory which we explored, however inadequately, in the previous chapter.

As we saw in that chapter the Newsom Committee recognized as a crucial determinant of educational planning 'the need of all boys and girls to develop capacities for thought and judgment, and to begin to arrive at some code of moral and social behaviour which is self-imposed' (§ 76). There seem to be echoes here of an ideal of 'personal autonomy based on reason'. These echoes are equally found reverberating in the chapter on *Spiritual and Moral Development* which also features in the opening section of the report. Religious education, it is claimed with obvious approval,

> can be, and usually is, given in a way which does justice to the mixed society in which we live, recognizing the range and degrees of religious belief and practice to be found in it, and respecting the right of the individual conscience to be provided with the material on which freely to decide its path (§ 167).

Yet, despite this acknowledgment of 'the mixed society in which we live' and other similar comments (e.g. 'the first factor to be reckoned with is that the staff will probably be divided in their philosophical and religious allegiance', § 158), nevertheless the stand-point of the whole chapter is clearly a Christian one.

> It is important that boys and girls should realise that 'going off the rails' does not involve for Christians losing the fellowship of the church, still less of forfeiting the love of God. There are other, and often graver, sins than those against chastity (§ 164).

> No Christian could for a moment rest content with an education which brought men face to face with a crucifixion but not with Christ. Religious instruction in accordance with any local education authority's agreed syllabus is instruction in the Christian religion. At once the subject becomes difficult and controversial. Not all teachers, not all parents, are Christians; some are avowedly opposed to religion; some feel that religion is only for children and some that it is only for adults – in the sense that boys and girls ought to be free to make up their minds when they grow up (this need provoke no dissent), and that therefore they ought not to be influenced one way or the other before they come to years of discretion (a corollary which Christians would neither accept as logical nor believe to be practicable). Some schools faced with this dilemma take refuge in equating Christianity with simple moral instruction. ... Faced with such evading tactics some Christians have felt that the 1944 settlement was a mistake and that no good could be expected of agreed syllabus religious instruction. We believe that they are wrong (§ 166f.).

A teacher cannot help his pupils unless he can put into words their ill-formulated problems and show them how Christians would set about solving them. He must know his Bible and its teaching, he must have thought about the relation of religion, and religious knowledge, to other fields of human activity and ways of knowing. A teacher may be a perfectly good church warden if he has solved his problems for himself in the terms in which these presented themselves half a generation ago, but on this basis alone he would not be adequately equipped to give religious instruction. For this his scholarship must be up to date, and he must move on the Christian frontiers of today (§ 169).

The 1944 Act in its religious settlement was based on faith that denominational differences could be resolved in such a way that they would not interfere with a real Christian education in county schools. That faith was justified (§ 172).

Even though these are selected passages, taken out of context, and it would therefore be possible to argue that they do not represent the whole argument of the chapter, these quotations nevertheless contain a sufficient number of statements to show that, at times at least, the Committee thought of themselves as Christians writing to Christians, and thought of RE as making a direct contribution to *Christian* education. They also thought of *Christian* education as being quite specifically the task of the nation's schools. In this they were in the full tradition of official educational thought which had existed over the previous century and more.

If the Newsom Report stood at a watershed, then the Plowden Committee found itself in the uncomfortable position of having one foot alongside the Newsom Report on the mountain top and the other one firmly in the 'open fields' below. Not surprisingly, the Committee split in two. The main body of the report contains phrases which indicate an understanding of RE in terms of initiation into Christian (or at least theistic) belief.

Young children need a simple and positive introduction to religion. They should be taught to know and love God and to

44

practise in the school community the virtues appropriate to their age and environment (§ 572).

Children should not be unnecessarily involved in religious controversy. They should not be confused by being taught to doubt before faith is established. Inevitably at some stage of the child's growth the truth of religious teaching will be questioned and a free judgment made as to its truth or falsehood. These judgments will only exceptionally be made by children of primary school age (§ 572).

And what sort of skills and expertise should teachers have so as to enable them to 'establish the faith' of their child pupils? The answer is given in terms fairly reminiscent of paragraph 169 of the Newsom Report (quoted above):

All teachers giving religious education should have some knowledge of biblical criticism. ... They should be able to relate the background and facts of the Christian revelation to situations which are within the children's experience, and so give their teaching vitality and greater relevance to the problems of life (§ 572,576).

And, in case some might doubt that the Christian revelation as such will be seen to be relevant to the problems of *primary school* life, reassurance on this point is forthcoming.

There will certainly be some stories about the life and teaching of Jesus which children can be taught at an early age. They may be led to find in him the expression of that which, in ways appropriate to their development, they have learnt to be good and true (§ 573).

It must be admitted that alongside these passages are a few comments which show that their authors did see the need for a slight tempering of this clearly committed position:

At this stage, as at any other, teachers should be sensitive to the feelings of children of parents who are non-Christian, agnostic or humanist as well as to those of Christian parentage (§ 575).

45

If children ask, as they will, whether stories are true, they should be given an honest answer by each teacher according to his lights. Neither the believing nor the non-believing teacher should try to conceal from his pupils the fact that others take a different view (§ 572).

However, there were certain members of the Committee who could not accept even this qualified position of commitment to a Christian basis of operation. These members, six in number, produced a 'note of reservation' which was appended to the main report. The main gist of this note runs as follows:

> Religious education, if it is taken at all seriously, is bound to involve theology; and theology ... cannot be properly adapted either to the understanding of children of this age or to the methods by which we are proposing that they should be taught. This does not mean that we wish children to grow up in ignorance of the content of Christian beliefs. ... They should be presented with the arguments in favour [of Christian theology] and the arguments against it and allowed to decide whether they find it credible. It is, however, absurd to suppose that the average, or even the very gifted child, is capable of appreciating these arguments before he is twelve years old. ... It may be argued that the main function of religious education in primary schools is to supply the children with a moral basis which they may not all be able to derive from their home life. What is true in this argument is that the school has a considerable part to play in inducing the children to accept an adequate set of moral, social and aesthetic values. ... On the other hand, we doubt if it is either necessary or desirable to insist on tying this aspect of education to theology. ... There is, of course, no reason why younger children should not be told Bible stories, just as, for very much the same cultural motives, they should be told the stories and legends of classical antiquity (pp. 489f.).

We will pick up some of these points later on, but first let us continue this review of 'official' positions regarding RE. Mention should be made, however briefly, of the Gittins Report on *Primary Education in Wales*. This was 'the Welsh Plowden', being published in the same year, 1967 (HMSO).

It might appear at first sight to have positioned itself much further out among the 'open fields' than Plowden did, because it calls for the abolition of the clause in the 1944 Education Act which 'requires' schools to provide RE. This was a call also made in the minority note of reservation in Plowden, but the reason for its appearance in the Gittins Report was in fact based on grounds totally opposite from those which were being defended by the Plowden minority. It was the belief of the Gittins Committee that 'even without statutory force an act of worship and the provision of religious education would be universally accepted and practised in the schools of Wales'. Not only would parents continue to want it for their children, but the schools themselves 'would earnestly and sincerely wish to continue this practice' (p. 369). In other words, the 1944 clauses were not in any basic way objectionable, merely unnecessary.

What is more, the character of the religious education which would be so enthusiastically provided in Welsh schools would be quite specifically that of an initiation process into the Christian community:

> In talking to our children in the primary school about religion, our first concern is not so much to pass on information (although this is necessary) but to establish attitudes – Christian attitudes towards God their Father, to Christ their Brother, to their neighbours, to the church (p. 370).

> The aim of using Bible stories is to teach right ideas about God and develop attitudes towards him. . . . The Bible is used to help children grow into a relationship with Christ so that they will wish to pattern their lives on his. The teacher first determines the attitude or response he desires to evoke and selects the gospel incident accordingly. The lesson to be drawn from the story must be evident so that the desired response is aroused (pp. 371f.).

In the outcome, then, the Gittins position reveals itself as being not post-Plowden, but entirely pre-Newsom in its understanding of the basic rationale of religious education.

47

The two most significant reports on RE to be published in the five years since 1967 will almost certainly prove to be the Durham Report and the Schools Council Working Paper No. 36. A number of other shorter 'committee documents' have emerged during this period, like the report of the special committee appointed by the Education Department of the BCC,[1] or the pamphlets *Religious Education, Present and Future*[2] and *Moral and Religious Education in County Schools*,[3] but most of what these have to say is either anticipated by, or incorporated into, the two longer reports. Both these reports, as will be seen, take up a position firmly established on the 'open fields' of the post-Newsom era.

The Durham Commission was set up in 1967 (by the Church of England Board of Education and the National Society) 'to examine the whole field of religious education at a time when hitherto accepted presuppositions were being questioned, the aims of religious education reconsidered, and methods of teaching transformed'. Its members included educational administrators (both from within the Church and from the LEA world), academic theologians and educationists (both from universities and from colleges of education) and practising RE teachers and heads of schools. It was given complete independence from the bodies which set it up, and after more than two years' work under its chairman, the Bishop of Durham (the Right Reverend Dr I. T. Ramsey), published its report in 1970 under the title *The Fourth R* (National Society/SPCK).

The first two chapters are basically historical in nature. The first traces the development of RE in England, especially over the course of the previous century; the second traces the development of theology over the same period, and the implications of this development for religious education. Then, in the third chapter, the inter-relation of religious education and moral education are explored. The arguments in these early chapters will be referred to in more detail later in this book, but it is important even at this stage to recognize that the chapter on RE (at which we are going to look at some length) had been preceded by these other three chapters with their historical, theological and philosophical concerns.

The chapter on 'Religious education in schools with special reference to County Schools' (i.e. 'not Church Schools') opens with an examination of 'some arguments which have been used in the past to justify or to support the inclusion of RE on the school curriculum' (§ 192). The main arguments so examined are (1) that public opinion wishes it to be taught in school; (2) that our place in the cultural tradition of the West necessitates it, even if only for the sake of understanding our past (cf. the Plowden note of reservation); (3) that RE is an essential basis of moral education (cf. Plowden again). All three of these arguments are 'certainly not wholly to be discounted', but are not accepted as being of anything but 'supportive' value. What is felt to be the basic justification for the inclusion of RE within a school curriculum is the 'educational' argument, namely that RE 'is a subject with its own inherent educational value'. The nature of this inherent educational value is indicated in the following passage:

> Man is a creature who finds himself perplexed with the mystery of his existence. He knows that he is, and ponders why he is, what he is, and what he is for. From the start of recorded history he has sought to find answers to the enigma of his origin and destiny, he has puzzled about the meaning and purpose of his life. He has sought explanations for his pain, his suffering, and the fact of his finitude. He has sought value systems to provide dignity and direction to his life. The great religions of the world find their frame of reference within these ultimate questions which man has asked and continues to ask -- questions which are a part of the human condition.
>
> The existence of a religious interpretation of life is a fact of history and of present human experience. There are many millions of men and women throughout the world who find through their religious beliefs a deep meaning and purpose for their lives and a system of values by which their lives can be lived. There appears to be a 'spiritual dimension' in man's

nature which requires to be expressed by 'religion' of one kind or another. By religion we mean some pattern of belief and behaviour related to the questions of man's ultimate concern. For some it is an Eastern religion; for some it is Christianity; for others it is one of the secular creeds of the West, for example Marxism; for others it is agnostic humanism; for many it may be little more than moral stoicism. Man seems to have to find 'a faith to live by', however noble, or simple, or debased. Young people share in the human condition. They should have some opportunity to learn that religion is a feature of this condition, and for some men a deeply significant area of human knowledge and experience (§ 204f.).

The grounds of the educational argument also become apparent if one looks at the implications of constructing a school curriculum in which religion (however broadly defined) were to find no place.

Religious education has its place on the school curriculum because it draws attention to a significant area of human thought and activity. A curriculum which excluded religion would seem to proclaim that religion has not been as real in men's lives as science, or politics, or economics. By omission it would appear to deny that religion has been and still is important in man's history (§ 211).

Having rejected non-educational reasons for pursuing RE in the schools of the country, and having established an educational rationale, *The Fourth R* then goes on to look at aims and objectives.

If religious education is placed in this general educational context, what should be its aim? The aim of religious education should be to explore the place and significance of religion in human life and so to make a distinctive contribution to each pupil's search for a faith by which to live. . . . The teacher is thus seeking rather to initiate his pupils into knowledge which he encourages them to explore and appreciate, than into a system of belief which he requires them to accept. To press for acceptance of a particular faith or belief system is the duty and privilege of the churches and other similar religious bodies. It

50

is certainly not the task of a teacher in a county school. If the teacher is to press for any conversion, it is conversion from a shallow and unreflective attitude to life. If he is to press for commitment, it is commitment to the religious quest, to that search for meaning, purpose and value, which is open to all men (§ 215–17).

The report, as was suggested above, clearly aligns itself with those educationists who place a central emphasis on the autonomy of their pupils. On the evidence of the above passages the members of the Durham Commission certainly could not be brought under Dearden's condemnation of ecclesiastical educators implied in his comment that the ideal of autonomy 'is opposed to any kind of authoritarian dictation or imposition, whether by parties, priests or public pressures'.[4] Nor is the report open to the charge of shifting its ground towards 'authoritarian imposition' when it makes the further point that 'the content of the RE curriculum in this country should consist mainly of the exploration of the literature and beliefs of the Christian faith' (§ 214). The important thing to recognize is that they advocate this concentration on Christianity not for sectarian reasons, as it were, but for purely practical educational reasons.

> All serious religious thought and experience has arisen within a tradition and cannot be understood apart from it. Hence there cannot be a religious education which is concerned simply with religion as such. It would be educationally unrealistic to propose that all pupils in the schools of England and Wales should study the Bible and, *as well*, the *Qur'an*, the *Bhagavad-gita*, the *Upanisads*, and the Buddhist scriptures. This would inevitably lead to extreme superficiality, even if there were enough teachers possessing the relevant qualifications. Religious education, to be of any value, must involve the thorough study of some particular religion (§ 213).

> The kind of understanding which is involved in religious education can be achieved only if pupils study the religious tradition or traditions of their own particular culture. For the great majority of pupils in England and Wales this is the Christian faith (§ 212).

51

There then follows a significant footnote:

> We fully recognize that Jewish parents will wish their children to be educated in the Jewish faith. We further recognize that the parents of some immigrant children will wish them to be taught their particular faith.

Perhaps it is a sign of the speed at which the final drafting had to be done that this point should have to appear in a footnote, and that it should be couched in terms of parental wishes rather than being grounded in educational necessity. For the whole gist of the argument in these paragraphs is that for educational reasons the religion on which greatest emphasis should be placed is that religion with which the pupils are already most familiar. It is the fact of its familiarity that makes it the most appropriate educational channel for exploring 'the place and significance of religion in human life and so making a distinct contribution to each pupil's search for a faith by which to live'. Unlike the Gittins Report, the Durham Report did not see the outcome of RE as being necessarily, or even optimally, membership of the Christian community, or even acceptance of a Christian view of life. The most that is being specifically cultivated in the field of thought is 'an understanding of the religious interpretation of life' (§ 209); in the field of attitudes the most that can legitimately be attempted is 'conversion from a shallow and unreflective attitude to life' or, in positive terms, 'commitment to that search for meaning, purpose and value, which is open to all men' (§ 217).

The fact that this 'search for meaning etc.' was described in the report as 'the religious quest' upset some humanist reviewers, and it must be admitted that the term 'religion' is not used with perfectly consistent meaning throughout these paragraphs. Where the report calls for the establishment of 'an understanding of the religious interpretation of life' among the pupils in our schools, then it is using 'religious' in its normal, conventional meaning. So it is when it claims that 'a curriculum which excluded religion would seem to proclaim that religion has not been as real in men's lives as science, or politics, or economics' (§ 211). On the other hand the report itself defines religion at one point as 'some pattern of belief and behaviour related to the questions of man's ultimate concern' (§ 205), and goes on quite specifically, as we have seen, to include Marxism, agnostic humanism and moral stoicism among such 'patterns of belief and behaviour'. This is certainly a very different definition of religion from the conventional meaning of the word, and this inconsistency of usage has inevitably given rise to certain misunderstandings.

The other main document we have yet to consider (the Schools Council Working Paper 36, *Religious Education in Secondary Schools*, Evans/Methuen 1971) tried to avoid such misunderstandings by grappling with the problem fairly near the beginning of its argument.

> There are two distinct but related fields open for exploration in the study of religion. For convenience these may be referred to as 'explicit' religion and 'implicit' religion. Explicit religion is religion as a phenomenon; implicit religion resides in those elements of secular experience – like wonder, guilt, and love – which evoke questions about life's ultimate significance, its values, meaning and purpose (p. 19).

This distinction between 'implicit' and 'explicit' religion became a central feature of the structure round which the whole document was built.

The working paper was the product of the team staffing the Schools Council Project on RE in Secondary Schools, based on the University of Lancaster, and was an attempt to set out the rationale underlying the subsequent production of certain curriculum materials for religious education. Unavoidably it also found itself exploring a number of related issues thrown up by the contemporary educational scene, such as the question of 'procedural neutrality' in the classroom and the extent to which the Christian RE teacher could function *as a Christian* in the classroom. Before returning to this latter point (which is of course the central theme of this chapter) let us look briefly at the argument of the first section of the paper.

Having examined a variety of answers to the question 'Why study religion in schools?', the paper then asks whether it is 'possible for teachers to be objective in dealing with such an emotionally charged subject as religion'. It suggests that there have been three approaches to RE, each of which implies a different answer to this question: (1) the 'confessional' or dogmatic approach; (2) the anti-dogmatic approach; (3) the 'educational' or undogmatic approach. These short, descriptive titles are annotated as follows:

1. This begins with the assumption that the aim of RE is intellectual and cultic indoctrination.

2. This rules out the subjective element from RE and conceives it as an academic exercise, dispassionate and objective.

3. This sees the aim of RE as the promotion of understanding. It uses the tools of scholarship in order to enter into an empathic experience of the faith of individuals and groups. It does not seek to promote any one religious viewpoint but it recognizes that the study of religion must transcend the merely informative (p. 21).

The third of these three approaches is the one favoured by the working paper because it 'pays due regard to the subjective element in religion' (by the use of 'imaginative participation') yet avoids 'mere subjectivism' or any assumption that 'true understanding' of religion can only spring from 'emotional involvement leading to commitment'. Not that the possibility of commitment by the pupil is ruled out; the paper quotes, approvingly, from an essay by P. H. Phenix:

Objectivity is not achieved by rising above the life of conviction into a realm of cool rational detachment. It is attained rather by the controlled deployment of one's own affective and conative life in the pursuit of sympathetic understanding of the inner life of other persons. ... Critical intelligence is fostered best in schools where studies are not regarded as exercises for the detached mind, but as opportunities for the development of responsible commitments by the whole person.[5]

Clearly this 'objectivity-with-commitment' of Phenix's is a long way from 'mere subjectivism'. Commitment certainly does involve discernment, and discernment is a way of seeing a particular situation or (in other words) a way of interpreting a particular set of percepts. This cannot but involve a considerable element of subjective response and decision-making. Nevertheless objectivity can still be preserved within one's commitment if three conditions are observed: (a) that 'the possibility of alternative patterns of interpretation' is admitted; (b) that 'schemes for the critical evaluation of alternatives' are pursued; and (c) that this is done within 'an atmosphere of academic freedom'.

Having, in this way, argued that one is indeed able to deal with religion in the classroom 'objectively' and still do justice to the subjective element within it, the paper then goes on to examine two ways of constructing this 'educational' approach. These two ways the paper associates respectively with the names of Harold Loukes (Reader in Education at the University of Oxford) and Ninian Smart (Professor in Religious Studies at the University of Lancaster).[6]

The first of these two ways of pursuing objective (or 'open') RE is described by the working paper as follows: 'an unrestricted personal quest for meaning in life in terms of actual experience, assisted by dialogue between pupil and teacher' (p. 34). This is obviously reminiscent of the definition of 'implicit' religion which came early in the paper ('it resides in those elements of experience which evoke questions about life's meaning'). Because of this, Loukes' way of approach is dubbed the 'implicit' or 'personal quest' approach.

The second way of pursuing an open educational approach to RE is to attempt the study of 'explicit' religion, but to attempt this from what the paper calls a 'phenomenological' standpoint. This latter label is being widely used in current writing about RE, in some cases with quite intentional reference to the philosophical school deriving from the work of Husserl, in other cases with no such reference being apparently intended at all. But rather than pursue this rather academic question any further at this point, it would probably be better simply to look at a later passage from the working paper to see precisely what its authors intended by the phrase:

Traditionally, in western education, a religion has been treated chiefly as a system of beliefs with an associated code of conduct. This is perhaps the chief reason why the study of 'comparative religions' has almost always been relegated to the final years of secondary schooling, when powers of abstract thinking have developed. But such an approach to religion is terribly inadequate. Religions have many aspects, some of which may be studied at quite an early age, and all of which must be studied if true understanding free from distortion is the aim of education. For example, when studying a given religion, one might distinguish first the 'observable' aspects – ritual, custom, buildings, books, etc. One might then study the teaching of the religion, the ideas and beliefs which underlie the observable aspects. After this one could go on to discover what these external phenomena mean to the people involved in and committed to the religion – the 'experiential' or existential aspect. In fact, without this data, a true understanding and appreciation of the religion would be impossible.

Smart emphasizes that religion is multi-dimensional. It has, in fact, six major dimensions:

(1) Doctrinal
(2) Mythological
(3) Ethical

These three dimensions together represent the general standpoint and world view of a religion, but they are not likely to come to life and be properly understood unless they are seen in their context – and that context is the living practice of the faith. This in turn has three dimensions:

(4) Ritual
(5) Experiential
(6) Social

56

These six 'dimensions of religion' are interrelated and inter-dependent. So long as this is borne in mind, and the inter-relations traced, they suggest six different starting-points for the study of a given religion (pp. 47f.).

The conclusion of this review of the two ways of approaching 'open' RE comes in chapter 4 of the working paper:

> We incline to the view that religious education must include both the personal search for meaning and the objective study of the phenomena of religion. It should be both a dialogue with experience and a dialogue with living religions, so that the one can interpret and reinforce the other.

To round off this stage of its argument the paper then lists what it sees as the main strands in the widespread con-temporary consensus regarding the aims of religious educa-tion:

> RE seeks to promote awareness of religious issues, and of the contribution of religion to human culture in general; it seeks to promote understanding of religious beliefs and practices, it also aims to awaken recognition of the challenge and prac-tical consequences of religious belief. Like all liberal education it is concerned that such awareness and understanding should be founded on accurate information, rationally understood and considered in the light of all relevant facts (p. 44).

The purpose of this chapter so far has been to give an ac-count of the main arguments, assertions and recommenda-tions to be found in the major 'committee documents' of the past decade which have dealt with religious education. What should by now be apparent is that over this decade there has been a fundamental shift in our understanding of what sort of process religious education ought to be. It is not just a question of new methods, or even just of new content, but of new aims, a new rationale. This shift in understanding is well illustrated by the phrase from the Durham Report which claims that the new-style teacher of RE is 'seeking rather to initiate his pupils into knowledge which he encourages them to explore and appreciate, than into a system of belief which he requires them to accept' (§ 216). Not that the RE teacher of the future is to have no further concern with the question of what his pupils believe. Far from it. The purpose served by the 'exploration of religion' is 'to make a distinctive contribution to each pupil's search for a faith by which to live' (§ 215). It is not merely to satisfy curiosity or extend cultural horizons.

This view of RE is also clearly set out in another Schools Council publication, *Humanities for the Young School Leaver: An Approach through Religious Education.*[7] Here the role of the RE teacher is described as follows:

> He poses and invites questions about the meaning of human life, and of the world in general. Is there meaning and purpose in the universe as a whole? And what difference to our attitudes and behaviour in particular circumstances does the answer to the general question make? The teacher will examine this inquiry with the aid of Christian and non-Christian statements. He will also examine the alternative – that there is no ultimate meaning in existence – and its implications. He will examine the nature of belief, and the necessity for making a choice of believing; for to say: 'I do not choose at all' is a denial of human status. The choice itself remains the pupil's own; and the teacher should not measure the success of his teaching by the extent to which his pupils agree with him. What he is called on to do, as a teacher, is to make clear the available choices, and the grounds thereof; and to help his pupils make their choices and face the consequences of making them (p. 11).

This passage could well be taken as the charter of what is now almost universally referred to as 'open-ended' RE. Success is judged not in terms of the positions finally adopted, but in terms of the quality of movement which led up to the adoption of these positions. Or, to put it in more immediately relevant concepts, it could well be regarded as a successful outcome of one's RE teaching if all one's pupils emerged with beliefs differing widely among themselves and differing totally from one's own. The only criteria applicable are that each one should have chosen his belief freely, knowledgeably, responsibly and consistently.[8]

Now one must ask whether a Christian RE teacher can apply these criteria to his own position and responsibly and consistently accept religious education as an 'open' process and operate according to the presuppositions we have been presented with in the passages quoted above. As was noted above, this is a question which Working Paper 36 raises in a short chapter among its closing pages. Two aspects of the question are identified, the commitment of the Christian to witness to his faith at all times, and the desire of the Christian teacher to provide 'the best education possible' for his pupils. (This might well be interpreted by many Christian teachers as an education which brings children within the Christian fold and so provides them with 'that peace which the world cannot give'.)

The working paper answers the first of these points by distinguishing two forms of Christian witness, 'silent witness' (through the quality of one's living) and 'proclamation'. The latter, it argues, is as inappropriate to the role of a Christian teacher in a 'secular' county school as it would be to a Christian car-salesman. What is more, it is as inappropriate to the role of the Christian RE teacher as it would be to the role of the Christian maths teacher. To say this, of course, does not rule out the need for the Christian teacher to maintain his 'silent witness' at all times. Possibly this silent witness may be instrumental in bringing some pupils to an acceptance of the Christian faith, but this will be purely incidental to the actual process of RE, which will not have this particular end in view at all. The RE teacher may well be quite legitimately helping his pupils in their search for faith, but on the question of *which* faith, the process must be an open-ended one.

The second aspect of the problem (the question of the Christian teacher wanting to provide 'the best' for his pupils) is approached in a way which really leads us to the heart of the whole issue. By what criterion, it is asked, is one judging what is 'best', and how certain can one be that one's judgment is right?

> The criterion of truth and knowledge by which we normally operate is the criterion of what is open to human reason. In religious conviction there is an element not open to human reason and rational investigation. Christianity must, therefore, be presented as 'what Christians believe', not 'what is the case' (p. 93).

Christianity, in other words, is only a matter of belief, of opinion. The Christian teacher is not really justified in saying 'In Christ, and in Christ alone, is peace'. Perhaps the world can provide an equal quality of peace after all. Or perhaps the most that can be found anywhere is only an *illusion* of peace. This view certainly seems to lie behind the suggestion (see p. 58 above) that RE teachers should examine the question of the meaning of life 'with the aid of Christian and non-Christian statements', and will also examine the alternative view 'that there is no ultimate meaning in existence'.

But *can* the Christian accept such an assertion? *Is* Christianity only a matter of belief, of opinion? Does not the fundamental Christian doctrine of revelation put Christian teaching on a quite different footing? In other words, does not Christianity claim for itself that it is *true*?

As we have already seen, the Christian understanding of revelation does not necessarily have to be embodied in a claim that God has 'explained' the nature of reality in a series of 'revealed truths' vouchsafed to his faithful servants and in turn relayed by them to us, so that it is simply a matter of saying 'He that hath ears to hear, let him hear'. The church through the ages, it must be granted, has maintained certain beliefs as being 'revealed truths' and as therefore being beyond the reach of reason. Not unnaturally Christians came to see these beliefs as possessing *more* truth than reason could attain to. But today our understanding of what we mean by revelation has shifted considerably. In the

60

first place, as the passages quoted from Temple in the previous chapter indicated, we would do better to think of God as revealing *himself* rather than as revealing propositional truths. This understanding of revelation has been more recently developed by Gabriel Moran in his book *God Still Speaks*:

> Revelation is not a 'thing', but exists only in present, continuing, conscious experience of people, that is in the relation of God and his people. ... The Bible is not a collection of revealed truths, divine pronouncements of words revealed from on high. God did not reveal the statements of the Bible; he revealed himself. ... The Word who is the fullness of God's revelation can be found by reading holy Scripture, but the Word cannot be confined to words. The Biblical words are the precipitate of a revelatory experience not fully expressible in words.[9]

If our understanding of the word 'revelation' has been modified in this way, then so has our understanding of the word 'truth'. Thanks to (and by reaction from) the excessively stringent interpretation of the term insisted on by the logical positivists earlier in this century, we have now come to see that ideas which used to be lumped together into the one category of 'true' are now better understood through a wide range of terms – 'experimentally demonstrable', 'logically necessary', 'personally experienced', etc. Alongside 'knowledge' we must now necessarily place 'awareness', 'insight', 'interpretation', not as better or worse forms of understanding, but as equally valid, inter-dependent forms of understanding (though they do, of course, become 'better' or 'worse' if one starts trying to substitute one for the other in inappropriate contexts). The old insistence that 'revealed truth' is not achievable by reason is now seen to be justified, but only in so far as it was an early attempt to differentiate categories of understanding. When it is taken to mean that revealed truth is 'better' than, 'truer' than, rationally acquired knowledge, then this leads to a total confusion of thought.

61

It is sometimes said that concepts such as 'insight', 'awareness', etc. cannot refer to the realm of publicly demonstrable knowledge. This may well be so, but it does not therefore follow that expressions of insight, etc. can be of no public benefit. The contemporary theologian will recognize that his task is no longer one of exposition, of publicly expounding eternally valid revealed truths; but he still has a vital public task, a task which is exploratory, not expository. He must take what the Durham Report calls 'the vehicles of vision of former days' (§ 85), what Moran might call 'the precipitate' of earlier revelatory experiences, and set these 'alongside the problems that emerge in our own day'. The outcome, it is to be hoped, is that 'the vision and the insight' conveyed through 'earlier stylings of the Christian faith' may be re-discovered in terms appropriate to our own times.

This dynamic view of revelation and what constitutes 'Christian truth' does, of course, make it quite possible for the Christian teacher to participate in 'open-ended' RE. In exploring (as opposed to expounding) Christian beliefs in company with his pupils he will be functioning both as an effective RE teacher, and as a Christian theologian (of however amateur a status!).

And it is his Christian commitment itself which makes this possible. As the Durham Report points out, it is by no means certain that open-ended RE could be justified on the basis of contemporary Islamic theology. Nor perhaps could fully open-ended RE be justifiable from the point of view of certain Hindu or Mahayanist theologies. But by virtue of his belief in the Incarnation the Christian, as *The Fourth R* says,

> is committed to the recognition of what is actually the case. Research into antiquity, discoveries in natural science, and the advances of reasoned thought are all relevant to a faith which claims not merely to contain true statements but to be the truth (§ 112).

To be the truth, to show men what actually is the case about human existence – this inevitably implies 'openness' to the whole complexity of the human situation, with all its possibilities for interpretation and varieties of self-understanding. Christian theology, because of its incarnational basis, shares with 'open' RE the need to 'provide for the possibility of a built-in self-criticism' in the exploration of its beliefs (§ 114). It is in this sense that we are to understand the aphorism of Meister Eckhart (which at first sight appears to be a total reversal of Dostoevsky's position referred to in the previous chapter): 'If God were able to backslide from truth I would fain cling to truth and let God go.'

This is the extent to which RE must be 'open'. When the RE teacher 'poses and invites questions about the meaning of life' he will not take as unchallengeable the presupposition that there *is* such a meaning. Whether any meaning which men may claim to have found has been truly found or simply invented will be left as an entirely open question.

To me this does not seem to place the Christian in any particular difficulty. The question 'to have faith, or to have no faith?' is not one which the Christian expects to be resolved solely by scientific demonstration or self-contained logical argument. This is an acknowledged feature of the religious quest, and should be accepted as such. What strikes me as being a much more difficult matter for the Christian RE teacher to come to terms with is the possible implication of open RE regarding faiths other than Christianity. It is logically necessary to accept the possible meaninglessness of existence as a valid alternative to the possibility of inherent meaning, but what does one say about the possible validity of alternative *grounds of meaning*? Is it logically necessary to accept all grounds of meaning, all faiths, as having equally the possibility of validity? Surely not, because once one has accepted the premise that there *is* meaning, then it would be quite possible, indeed likely, that this meaning is grounded in one characteristic of existence rather than another. The claim which has frequently been made that Christianity sets forth *the* truth about the significance of life, is a claim which is logically tenable, once the initial premise about the possibility of any significance at all is granted. And yet open-ended RE would seem to imply that all faiths are equally valid. Can the Christian teacher really accept such an implication, or must he insist on the uniqueness (and the superiority) of Christianity? If Christianity is not *the* truth, then why does he remain a Christian?

In his introduction to *Attitudes Toward Other Religions*,[10] Owen C. Thomas suggests that there have been two basic attitudes among Christians to other religions. One attitude regards other religions as 'simply idolatry and the creation of human self-assertion', the other sees them as 'honest human attempts to respond to the manifestation of God in nature and conscience'. It must be emphasized that even the second of these attitudes takes it as being self-evident that it *is* a manifestation of God to which men are responding, that there *is* meaning to be discovered. Even Troeltsch, whose position Thomas takes as typifying 'relativism' in its most fully worked-out form, still holds to the conviction that 'the impulse toward absolute objective truth' which man feels within himself is *not* simply the pursuit of a chimaera.

> All the historical religions are tending in the same direction, all seem impelled by an inner force to strive upward toward some unknown final height, where alone the ultimate unity and the final objective validity can lie. And, as all religion has thus a common goal in the Unknown, the Future, perchance in the Beyond, so, too, it has a common ground in the Divine Spirit ever pressing the finite mind onward toward further light and fuller consciousness.[11]

However, despite the assertion that 'final objective validity' does lie *somewhere*, by placing it in 'the Unknown, the Beyond' Troeltsch makes such validity possible only in terms of what John Hick has called 'eschatological verification'. The situation is somewhat like the well-known optical illusion caused by the drawing of a transparent cube. It is impossible to tell whether the cube is being viewed slightly from below or slightly from above, or whether it is turned slightly to the left or slightly to the right. Yet if it is a drawing of an *actual* cube, that cube must in reality be in one particular position, and not the other. The ambiguous drawing represents a real situation which is totally unambiguous. However (and here is the crux of the analogy), it is only when we are able to move from the two-dimensional to the three-dimensional that we can know with any assurance at all what that reality is. Troeltsch was arguing that we are at the moment confined, as it were, to the two-dimensional. Therefore the situation remains ambiguous:

> Between these two poles – the divine Source and the divine Goal – lie all the individual differentiations of race and civilization and, so far as human eye can penetrate into the future, it would seem probable that the great revelations to the various civilizations will remain distinct, in spite of a little shifting of their several territories at the fringes, and that the question of their several relative values will never be capable of objective determination.[12]

For what reasons, therefore, can the Christian hold to his own faith once he recognizes the relativity of the present (even if not of the final) situation? Troeltsch answered this question with the concept of 'inner validity':

> Christianity could not be the religion of such a highly developed racial group if it did not possess a mighty spiritual power and truth; in short, if it were not, in some degree, a manifestation of the Divine Life itself. The evidence we have for this is the evidence of a profound inner experience. This experience is undoubtedly the criterion of its validity, but, be it noted, only of its validity *for us*. It is God's countenance as revealed to us; it is the way in which, being what we are, we receive, and react to, the revelation of God. But this does not preclude the possibility that other racial groups, living under entirely different cultural conditions, may experience their contact with the Divine Life in quite a different way, and may themselves also possess a religion from which they cannot sever themselves so long as they remain what they are.[13]

C

Troeltsch wrote this in 1923, at a time when the cultural boundaries in the world still seemed pretty firmly drawn. Thirty or so years later, when the basic unity of the world had been much more clearly borne in upon us, when (to point to but a very trivial straw in the wind) the sitar was about to be adopted into the world of western pop-music, Arnold Toynbee was able to put forward an even more thoroughgoing version of the relativist position.

> If the world continues to grow together into a single family, objective judgments between different living religions will become in the course of time rather less difficult to make, as the unification of the world proceeds. I think one form that this unification will take will be a unification of our different cultural heritages. ... In contrast to the traditional state of religious affairs in which, almost automatically, one remained for life in the religious communion into which one had been introduced by the accident of being born in a particular place at a particular time, I think the tendency toward making a free choice of religion in grown-up life is likely to increase as the world grows closer together.... What then should be the attitude of Christians towards the other higher religions and their followers? I think that it is possible for us, while holding that our own convictions are true and right, to recognize that, in some measure, all the higher religions are also revelations of what is true and right. They also come from God, and each presents some facet of God's truth.[14]

As Thomas comments, in summarizing this point of view, 'All other religions are simply different paths to the same goal as Christianity. So which path you choose is only a matter of personal preference.' (This may be an over-simplification of the case which Toynbee was actually trying to present, but it is difficult to see how one can avoid eventually being driven into such a simply-stated position once one has taken as a starting point the sort of assertions which Toynbee makes in the above quotation, particularly in the final sentence.)

Thomas comments further, 'It is sometimes asserted that

all religions are equally true. But this would seem to be simply sloppy thinking, since the various religions hold views of reality which are sharply different if not contradictory.' At least, Thomas says, the exclusivist view of Christianity does 'take the problem of truth seriously'.

Not that every form of the exclusivist attitude denies the possibility that people from non-Christian cultures may 'experience contact with the Divine Life'. To avoid the completely relativist position one does not have to accept the view held by so many Victorian missionary hymn-writers:

> Through midnight gloom from Macedon
> The cry of myriads as of one,
> The voiceful silence of despair,
> Is eloquent in awful prayer,
> The soul's exceeding bitter cry,
> 'Come o'er and help us, (*dim*) or we die.'
> How mournfully it echoes on!
> For half the earth is Macedon.

Or again:

> From many an ancient river,
> From many a palmy plain,
> They call us to deliver
> Their land from error's chain.
> Can we, whose souls are lighted
> With wisdom from on high,
> Can we to men benighted
> The lamp of life deny?[15]

The middle ground between the fully relativist and the fully exclusivist position is occupied by those who believe, in some form or other, that Christianity is 'the purest and fullest manifestation' of God's revelation, and yet do not deny that other religions are also a manifestation of God's revelation, however imperfectly understood. On this view Christianity is seen as a 'definitive edition' of a manuscript whose earlier editions had been faulty in certain (but only in certain) particulars; or it is seen as a final refinement of a substance which had previously only existed in an impure form, but which nevertheless had been quarried from authentic ore, and had had all along the potentiality of further refinement within it.

Apparently running across this middle ground can be traced a path which runs from Barth through Brunner to Bonhoeffer. At one end the path seems as if it can lead only to the outright rejection of the other religions in favour of Christianity. As Brunner puts it:

> Christianity cannot admit that its faith is one species of the genus 'religion', or if it does so, only in the sense in which it regards itself as the true religion in contrast to the other false religions. To the outsider this looks like narrow-minded or fanatical intolerance; actually it is a necessary expression of sober truth.[16]

Brunner does not deny that God has revealed himself outside Christianity. He admits that 'even the most primitive religion is unintelligible without the presupposition of the universal revelation of God which has been given to all men through the Creation'. However, he insists that due to original sin this revelation has become overlaid with man's 'inveterate tendency to be absorbed in himself', and so man's religions have become 'daemonic distortions of the truth', have become in fact examples of 'man's effort to escape from God'.[17]

Man can only be saved from this daemonic distortion by a further, redemptive revelation. This, Brunner claims, was granted to man in Jesus Christ.

> Jesus Christ is both the Fulfillment of all religion and the Judgment on all religion. As the Fulfiller, He is the Truth which these religions seek in vain. ... From the standpoint of Jesus Christ, the non-Christian religions seem like stammering words from some half-forgotten saying. ... For Jesus Christ is not only the Fulfillment; He is also the Judgment on all religion. Viewed in His light, all religious systems appear untrue, unbelieving and indeed godless.[18]

68

It would not seem from this résumé of Brunner's argument so far that anyone holding his views could honestly participate in any open-ended form of RE such as has been advocated in the documents examined earlier in this chapter. But this is not in fact the end of Brunner's argument. The phrase 'the non-Christian religions' which appears in the passage above is somewhat misleading, 'for in Jesus Christ "the Christian religion" is judged as much as the other religions'. A true response to God's revelation 'can consist only in the fact that our trust is not in "religion" at all, but wholly and solely in that divine mercy which meets us in that revelation'. Because of this insistence on the principle of *sola fide* Brunner was able to write:

> All religion creates a gulf between the sacred and the secular; it is religion in contrast to the secular. In Jesus this contrast is explicitly denied; nothing is secular, all is sacred, for all belongs to God. Jesus rejects holy seasons, holy persons, holy places, specially holy acts, and indeed, too, the holy gods; for what the religions know as 'gods' are not truly holy, not truly divine. In Jesus the protest of the atheist against religion is also fulfilled.[19]

From here it is but a short step to Bonhoeffer and another short step to Christian secularity, and it looks as if we have followed the path right across 'the middle ground' and emerged at a point where one could take a full and honest part in open-ended RE after all. Certainly Thomas' résumé of the secularist position in the introduction to his book would seem to imply this.

> The advocates of Christian secularity see the world-wide process of secularization as the decisive fact of our time which challenges and threatens every world view. They also see secularization as the fruit of the Christian gospel. It is something to be welcomed, since it liberates man from all types of religious and metaphysical bondage, from the supremacy of fate, from the tyranny of cosmic powers, from the divinity of kings, and from the strictures of unquestioned ideologies. So

the proper Christian attitude toward other religions is not that they should be replaced by the Christian religion. Rather Christians should help the adherents of other religions to free themselves from those aspects of their religion and culture which inhibit their freedom and responsibility, and which have caused them to accept their lot fatalistically and to turn to the eternal world for religious solace.[20]

The Christian secularist will of course equally wish to help his fellow Christians free themselves from 'those aspects of religion and culture which inhibit their freedom and responsibility', and therefore would be able without difficulty to accept one of the basic premises of open-ended RE, inasmuch as 'it does not seek to promote any one religious viewpoint'. And yet he would not thereby have committed himself to an acceptance of all the implications of open-ended RE. The Christian secularist RE teacher would presumably not feel he had 'succeeded' if any of his pupils persisted in clinging to a highly other-worldly or fatalistic religious belief, whether such belief were in a Christian, Muslim, Hindu or any other form.

The Christian secularist does in fact hold an 'exclusivist' view of the truth, even though he is quite willing to treat Christianity (in its 'religious' form) on an equal basis with other religions. So the path which looked as if it led across the 'middle ground' to a final position of 'openness', turns out to have been traversing exclusivist regions the whole time.

I have dealt with this issue at some length because I suspect that at least a few of the eager supporters of open-ended RE are in fact Christian secularists who feel that their beliefs suit them automatically for teaching this type of RE. The truth is, however, that in such hands any RE would rapidly cease to be open-ended and could become simply a vehicle for secularist (albeit Christian secularist) propaganda. The secularist just as much as the fundamentalist needs to keep his exclusivist beliefs firmly in check if his RE teaching is to be truly open-ended.

But it is not only exclusivist Christians (of any type) who would fail to qualify *automatically* as teachers of open-ended RE. Any RE teacher who believed that Christianity was in *any* sense 'the fulfillment' or the 'final refinement' of other religions would not be happy if some of his pupils rejected Christianity and turned, say, to Buddhism or 'transcendental meditation'. Only if he is a thoroughgoing relativist can a Christian teacher unhesitatingly accept all the basic premises of open-ended RE. A Christian of any other persuasion has to take the specific step of deliberately setting on one side his own beliefs about the comparative value of other religions before he can start to teach from a properly open basis. It may only be a 'procedural' step, inasmuch as it is a suspension of his beliefs, not a permanent abandonment of them, but procedural or otherwise, it is a step which has to be taken.

Is the Christian teacher able to take such a step? The answer to this question will depend on the view of revelation which he holds. If he believes that God has revealed the truth in such a way that men can have 'knowledge' of it, then he will not accept that any teaching he is responsible for can in the final analysis be open-ended. He will feel impelled to teach the truth to his pupils. He will of course want to use the most effective means to this end and these may well include methods which appear to be 'open' methods, such as discussion, or comparative study of beliefs, but these will be employed solely to make his pupils more receptive to 'the truth' when it emerges, and he will not count his teaching as successful unless ultimately all his pupils come to see the truth as he sees it.

On the other hand, even if he firmly believes that the Christian 'vehicles of vision' offer the fullest *insight into* truth available to man, if he also believes that revelation leads to a new relationship rather than to new knowledge, then he will be content to work alongside his pupils exploring further his own insights at the same time as he encourages them to explore their own, and joining with them in the exploration of the insights of others. He will be prepared to say he has been successful, even if his pupils differ from him, as long as they have come to recognize that they too have embarked on a continuing exploration, a deepening of insights, and have not already attempted to settle behind fixed walls (either of belief or unbelief) such as would prevent any future movement or development of awareness.

Now is this a fully open-ended situation? In a real sense it is *not*. It is indeed a little reminiscent of the viewpoint, described by Thomas, whose adherents 'assert that any religion which denies that all religions are equally true is guilty of falsehood!' But then, no one is seriously advocating *complete* open-endedness. No one is suggesting that an RE teacher (or any teacher, come to that) could count himself successful if all his pupils became followers of Charles Manson or Alistair Crowley. As we saw in a previous chapter that the ideal of autonomy has to be qualified by certain 'conditions' so, too, open-endedness has to submit to certain enclosing criteria. It is not as if one were operating outwards in any direction from the centre of a sphere. Certain directions, certain planes of development are excluded by the need to observe such educational criteria as rational consistency, sufficient acquaintance with the relevant facts, and above all a general responsibility of judgment. Such criteria as these, then, indicate a definite range of direction along which exploration is to occur. To insist on open-endedness is not to seek to break down these guiding side-walls, but to ensure that any journey embarked on within these protective limitations is not cut short simply because someone in authority decrees that the final destination has now been reached.

NOTES

1. See Colin Alves, *Religion and the Secondary School*, SCM Press 1968, pp. 13–22.

2. HMSO 1969.

3. Social Morality Council 1970.

4. Dearden, *op. cit.*, pp. 48f.

5. P. H. Phenix, 'Religion in American Public Schools', in *Religion and Public Order*, University of Chicago Press 1965, pp. 87f. (quoted on pp. 22f. of Working Paper 36).

6. See e.g. H. Loukes, *New Ground in Christian Education*, SCM Press 1965 and N. Smart, *Secular Education and the Logic of Religion*, Faber & Faber 1968.

7. Published by Evans/Methuen Educational, 1969.

8. Compare John Wilson's criteria 'of moral rationality' in his *Introduction to Moral Education*, Penguin Books 1967, p. 93f.

9. Gabriel Moran, *God Still Speaks*, Burns & Oates 1967, pp. 19, 83, 88f.

10. Owen C. Thomas (ed.), *Attitudes Toward Other Religions*, SCM Press 1969.

11. From Ernst Troeltsch, 'The Place of Christianity among the World Religions', *Christian Thought: Its History and Applications*, University of London Press 1957. Quoted in Thomas, p. 89.

12. *Ibid.*, pp. 85ff.

13. *Ibid.*

14. From Arnold Toynbee, *Christianity Among the Religions of the World*, OUP 1958. Quoted in Thomas, pp. 163–5.

15. *Hymns Ancient and Modern*, Nos. 361 and 358.

16. From Emil Brunner, *Revelation and Reason: The Christian Doctrine of Faith and Knowledge*, SCM Press 1947, pp. 258ff. Quoted in Thomas, pp. 116ff.

17. *Ibid.*

18. *Ibid.*

19. *Ibid.*

20. Thomas, op. cit., p. 27.

4 Christianity in the School

Our enquiry into the nature of 'open RE' in the previous chapter brought us eventually to the assertion that although it must be fully open-*ended*, it is nevertheless not a completely open situation that is being advocated. There are certain criteria to be observed, certain standards to be met, certain values to be preserved. These provide the guidelines within which the open-ended journey of discovery may proceed.

But how are these guide-lines set up? How are the pupils made aware of the criteria? How do they come to appreciate the standards and values that provide the framework of the whole enterprise? Part of the answer to these questions obviously lies with the methods and general approach used in the RE classroom, but an even larger part lies with the work carried on in the *other* areas of the curriculum, and with what is known as the general *ethos* of the school.

Recognition of the importance of rationality in one's approach to the world will of course be built up in the mathematical and scientific work done in the school, and also in the work in the 'social studies' area (however this may be timetabled). But it will also be affected by the way the life of the school is organized, and by the way patterns of behaviour are controlled. If there are a large number of petty rules which appear to have no rational justification, and above all if personal authority (of staff or of senior pupils) is exercised in an authoritarian manner, then rationality will be devalued in the eyes of the whole school. If a child is being constantly told (however subtly or politely) 'You do this because I say so' (or 'because it's a rule'), then that child will not be encouraged to exercise rationality in his own thinking.

Similarly with the matter of consistency. If the child knows that what is said in 'official pronouncements' is either ignored or openly rejected by senior members of the school community, then he will not be much impressed by demands that he should be consistent in his own thinking and behaviour. (I am not referring here, of course, to honest differences of opinion between any member of staff and the 'official line' on a specific issue, but to the situation where, for example, high ideals are publicly vaunted although they are noticeably absent from actual practice.)

Or again, there is 'concern for facts'. It is no good urging pupils to make themselves 'sufficiently acquainted with the relevant facts' when they are trying to decide issues in science, history, RE or whatever, if at the same time one is in the habit of refusing to listen to the pupil's version of apparent misdemeanours and simply makes one's disciplinary judgments on the basis of 'general reputation'.

But it is not only in matters of discipline and the exercise of authority that concern for standards and values is communicated. The whole area of 'school activities' is of considerable importance in this process. The amount of attention officially given to school sporting events both reflects and conveys concern for certain values. This is true not only in general terms, but in quite specific ways as well. If regular announcements are made about the successes of the school football team, while nothing at all is said about the table-tennis or the chess team, this is an indication of the value placed upon the different activities. Similarly there is a real significance in the amount of time and attention the school is prepared to give to cultural activities, not merely on the timetable (though this too has its significance) but by way of school concerts, school plays, school exhibitions. All activities of this sort can absorb a vast amount of time and effort, but if those responsible convey to the rest of the school that this is time and effort well spent, then a very important step has been taken in the communication of values.

What is more, with cultural activities of this sort, communication of values occurs not only through the *fact* that concerts, plays, exhibitions, etc. occur, but through the material chosen for these occasions. Obviously when the purpose of, say, an exhibition is to show work done *by* the pupils, then the criteria of selection will depend on questions such as 'Is the material to be representative of the whole range of pupils? Is one purpose of the exhibition to encourage the less talented by including some of their work?' But when already existing work is being selected, for performance or display, then the question of standards and values becomes paramount. Is it enough to select music for a concert simply on the grounds that it is sufficiently easy for the performers to tackle, and equally easy on the ears of the audience? If these were the only criteria employed then every school concert would be a sort of *Junior Show Time*, or a mixture of *Country meets Folk* and *The Palm Court*, possibly with a few rugger songs thrown in to please the hearties. The choosing of material for school plays can be even more important for displaying and developing values within a school. A school which put on nothing but Whitehall farces year after year would be saying something quite significant to its pupils about standards and values. So would a school which concentrated solely on Greek tragedy. For the moment I am not suggesting that the one situation is necessarily better than the other, or that either is worse than one where a more mixed bill of fare is offered. What I *am* saying is that one can gain a very clear impression of the fundamental beliefs of a community from its choice of material for public performance. It may be quite a mistaken impression (if, for example, there had been no co-ordinated policy at all, but a series of quite haphazard choices appeared to the outside eye to add up to a significant pattern), but the point is that this is the impression which has been gained. A school should therefore always be asking itself what *are* the values that it wishes to see publicly displayed and supported.

Of course the problem in so many schools today is that there appears to be no overall consensus as to what this pattern of values would comprise. R. F. Dearden, whose book on *The Philosophy of Primary Education* we referred to at some length in the second chapter, puts the problem this way:

> Our society presents not just one monolithic world-view, but many, often competing, views as to what is valuable in human life. And in respect of this plurality of values a school, which in practice the great majority of children are legally compelled to attend, ought not to be in any way partisan as between these various ideals of life. With what values, then, can the school be concerned in its educational function?[1]

Unfortunately Dearden answers this question on the basis of a rather narrow interpretation of 'educational function', and concentrates to a large extent on what can best be described as 'work done in the classroom'. Yet this problem of the 'pluralistic background' to a school's responsibilities in the field of values is even more pressing on the broader plane of the ethos of the school and the school's corporate activities.

To revert, for the moment, to the area of discipline and regulations; the Newsom Report, it will be recalled, also noted that 'society is divided' on many issues of value, and especially on issues of moral value. For example:

> Those personal situations which most perplex adolescent boys and girls are, however, situations about which there is no universal contemporary agreement. The challenging feature of their lives is now the sexual instinct which is at its most potent in these years. A hundred years ago nearly all good men would normally have given the same answers to the problems which beset the young immediately in their courtship habits and prospectively in their conception of the marriage relation. To-day Christians and many agnostics would still agree in their

attitudes, but it would be stupid to deny that there are profound differences in society about pre-marital intercourse and about the permanence of marriage, or that these must be reflected in many staffrooms. Tensions there must be if the questions of boys and girls are heard and answered and not suppressed – tensions, perhaps, within the staff of a school and tensions between school and home (§ 164).

However, despite these acknowledged differences of viewpoint within society, the members of the Newsom Committee felt that adolescent pupils needed to be offered guidance, that it would 'be wrong to leave the young to fend for themselves' in this situation. The Committee were also prepared to suggest what this guidance should actually be:

> For our part we are agreed that boys and girls should be offered firm guidance on sexual morality based on chastity before marriage and fidelity within it. We believe, too, that this is predominantly the standpoint of the schools (*ibid.*).

This was written in 1963. Could the same be said today? Certainly there have been loud voices raised of late in protest against the giving of guidance in these definite terms. The article on sex education in *Let's Teach Them Right*[2] complained against the all-pervasiveness of 'moralistic' books on sex for use in schools. There have also been some notable attempts since then to produce material which was a-moral in its outlook, e.g. Dr Martin Cole's film *Growing Up*. However, it is difficult to say how widely such an approach is being welcomed by the teaching profession as a whole. Dr Cole's professedly a-moral position was certainly regarded as an *im*moral one by many teachers and educational administrators who saw his film.

As far as the views of the pupils are concerned we do have some fairly conclusive evidence of a shift of opinion since 1963. In that year Derek Wright and Edwin Cox carried out a survey among just over 2,250 sixth-formers, using a questionnaire which included a question on the rightness/wrongness of premarital sexual intercourse. The range of judgment displayed by the sixth-formers is indicated in the following table of percentage responses:

	always wrong	usually wrong	sometimes wrong	never wrong
Boys	28·6	27·6	20·5	10·2
Girls	55·8	25·2	6·6	2·4

(The remaining percentages were 'undecided')

Wright and Cox repeated this survey in the same schools in 1970. The percentage figures for the premarital sexual intercourse question on this occasion were as follows:

	always wrong	usually wrong	sometimes wrong	never wrong
Boys	10·3	12·8	30·4	33·7
Girls	14·6	19·5	30·0	17·7

Admittedly these figures are related to the realm of theoretical judgments, to moral *belief*. There is no necessary correlation with the realm of behaviour. As Wright suggests in his commentary on the figures,[3] the sixth-formers of today are not condoning promiscuity; they are saying no more than 'provided the couple love each other and are responsible it is no one's business to pass moral judgments on them'. Nevertheless, a shift of opinion as clearcut as this one has been will obviously remove at least one restraint (disapproval by one's peers) from any couple who wished to engage in premarital intercourse, even at school. Should the school itself counter this, by stressing the importance of chastity even more than it may have done in the past, or should it refuse to take a 'partisan' view on the matter (to use Dearden's term) and (again in Dearden's words) lay it down that in this area 'the teacher's function is no more than that of disclosure of possible ideals' leaving the matter as an entirely open one in which the pupil must exercise his own unguided choice?

Now it seems to me that a very important distinction needs to be made here, namely the distinction between theoretical exploration of the issues involved and the practical arrangements governing actual behaviour in the related area. It has been suggested, quite seriously, that the sexual situation in society has altered so completely in the past few years that this should be reflected in the regulations governing school life (especially in the sixth form), even to the extent of providing an intercourse-room for use at break time. (This, it is argued, would at least prevent any embarrassment which might still possibly arise should couples desire to give sexual expression to their love in the playground or in the changing rooms.)

What would be the reaction of a Christian headteacher faced with such a suggestion? If he were faced in a discussion group with the theoretical suggestion that perhaps chastity was outmoded, he would, I feel, be completely justified, as a Christian, in examining this as a perfectly open question, exploring without pre-judgment both the arguments which might seem to support chastity and those which might seem to support free love, and even those which seem to support unrestrained sexuality of a totally physical kind with no emotional involvement whatsoever. All the arguments about 'open-ended RE' in the previous chapter would apply here also. However, the issue before us is not one of theoretical discussion, but of practical decision. Must he, to remain consistent, be 'open' on this issue also?

The first point he would have to decide is whether he thought chastity, or at least sexual restraint, was a necessary corollary of his view, as a Christian, of man's nature and potential. (Cf. the discussion of Temple's phrase 'The right of the individual to be himself' in chapter 2.) If he did think this – and it will be obvious from the drift of the argument that I believe that he *ought*, as a Christian, to think this – then he has to make the further, and crucial, decision as to whether he has the right to make this personal belief the ground of his response to the suggestion put before him, a response which could well limit the freedom of action of people who do not share that belief.

Here we are up against the further question of the role of the headteacher in a school. Is he there as an administrator to ensure that the majority view on any matter is put into effect as easily and quickly as possible, or does he have the actual responsibility of deciding not simply what is the majority view, but what is the *best* view on any matter? All sorts of other questions cluster round this one. If (as has been traditional) the head has a clear responsibility for making the decision as to what is best, then how far can such a system be described as democratic, either where the staff is concerned, or indeed where the pupils themselves are concerned? To what extent *should* a school be democratic in its operation? Space does not allow us to pursue all the implications here. We must simply assume that heads will continue to be appointed with specific responsibility to make (not merely carry out) decisions.

We must also assert that in making these decisions it is perfectly justifiable that a head's personal beliefs should colour his judgments. In *The Fourth R* the theoretical bases of moral education are examined (in the third chapter) and this conclusion is reached:

'Openness' cannot mean 'not having any presuppositions'. . . . It must mean 'not being doctrinaire, being ready to consider arguments against one's own position'. As such it is compatible with having and with communicating a definite position which one is prepared to defend (§ 158).

And in an appendix to the report, Basil Mitchell makes the further point that 'educators who scrupulously refrain from introducing any bias into the educational process will not thereby ensure that their pupils escape bias, only that the bias is imparted by other agencies'. This could be rephrased to apply to the particular issue under consideration: head-teachers who scrupulously refrain from allowing their personal beliefs to influence any decision they take regarding their pupils will not thereby ensure that their pupils are free of all influence from personal beliefs, only that it is *other people's* personal beliefs that place limits on their 'freedom to be themselves'.

Once again that phrase of Temple's needs to be unpacked, if only to remind us that the alternative to the Christian understanding of 'being oneself' is not a completely neutral state of 'actually being oneself' but must be someone else's *understanding* of what 'being oneself' involves. As the earlier Schools Council paper mentioned above puts it: 'Atheism and other forms of so-called disbeliefs are not *dis*beliefs but beliefs.'[4] No man can avoid basing his thought and pattern of behaviour on a whole substructure of presuppositions. What is important is not that he should try to dispense with this substructure (he cannot), but that he should be fully aware of what exactly his presuppositions are. As we saw earlier in the chapter, this applies as much to communities as it does to individuals, and it applies especially (despite all the difficulties) to communities whose concern is an educational one.

Mention has already been made of the important implications of 'school activities', those occasions when events are arranged in the name of the whole school. Although sporting events and cultural events are perhaps the most obvious of these 'school activities' to the eye of the outside observer, in actual fact the most frequent event in this category (and therefore, potentially at least, the most important) is the school assembly. Readers of the Newsom Report might well be forgiven if they failed to recognize this fact, because this particular report places assembly within a very narrow context. Despite a deliberate concentration on 'the school's communal life', to the extent of three whole chapters, the report spends precisely one paragraph on the matter of school assembly, and treats it there in surprisingly non-educational terms:

> We have visited many schools and taken part in their morning assembly. We can say with conviction and gratitude that we

have very often been impressed by the reality which has marked these services. Corporate worship is not to be thought of as an instrument of education – though it is that – but as a time in which pupils and teachers seek help in prayer, express awe and gratitude and joy, and pause to recollect the presence of God (§ 174).

On the other hand the Plowden Report, following the sort of framework suggested by the 1944 Education Act, looked at 'the Act of Worship' under the heading of *Religious Education* (in the chapter on *Aspects of the Curriculum*) rather than in the chapter on *The Child in the School Community*. It did, however, have a general paragraph on 'The School Community' introducing the section on 'the Act of Worship' and it had this to say on the subject itself:

> We believe that the Act of Worship has great value as a unifying force for the school and that in it children should find, in brief moments, a religious expression of their life in school.... In a school of mixed religious or non-religious backgrounds, it is essential that the assembly should be conducted in such a way that as large a part of the school community as possible, both teachers and children, can take part in it without offence being given to anyone's conscientious scruples.... The Act of Worship should illuminate personal relationships and introduce children to aesthetic and spiritual experience. It can derive material from other than Christian sources (§ 570f.).

The differences between these two passages are obvious, and significant. The Newsom Committee spoke as if there was little difference between a school assembly and a church service, or between a school community and a church congregation. They also gave only very grudging acknowledgment to the fact that the events of school assembly might have educational consequences, as opposed to ecclesiastical or pietistic ones. In contrast, the Plowden Committee seemed anxious to play down the religious aspects of assembly (even though they felt obliged, for legal reasons, to call it 'the Act of Worship' most of the time). There seem to have been two reasons for this shift of emphasis: the first was a recognition that the role of assembly within a school could not be confined to its purely devotional aspects; the second was a deep concern for those members of the school community ('both teachers and children') who were unable to respond to these devotional aspects, especially if these were confined to Christian modes of expression.

The note of reservation at the end of the Plowden Report, as would be expected, went much further and argued that 'assembly should be legally dissociated from the Act of Worship'. Unfortunately they gave no indication of what sort of occasion they felt 'assembly' should in future become, but at least they opened up future discussion by pointing to the possibility of dissociating two elements which had earlier appeared to most people to be indissolubly fused.

In their report published in the following year, the members of the special committee set up by the Education Department of the British Council of Churches accepted the Plowden shift of emphasis, though they still saw 'assembly' as definitely incorporating an element which was identifiable as 'worship' in some sense of the word:

> We believe that the morning assembly can have great value of a spiritual kind beyond any justification it may deserve as an expression of corporate life. As many as possible should be encouraged to take part as fully as possible in it. This means in our judgment that, while the assembly will usually be Christian, at other times it will be a sincere expression of spiritual values which are not avowedly Christian, though the Christians among the staff and pupils will give them more profound significance in the light of their religious understanding. We think it reasonable to assume that the great majority of teachers and pupils would be prepared to take part in daily assemblies which had this latitude of expression.[5]

This approach to the problem, the 'opening-up', rather than the abandonment, of traditional forms, was taken further by the Durham Report. Altogether the report devoted almost forty paragraphs to the question of *Worship in County Schools*, and the problem was seen as being so complex that no brief concluding recommendation was felt to be appropriate or adequate. As a result the general list of recommendations with which the report ends contains no recommendations on school assembly but simply refers the reader back to the chapter in which the arguments are set out at length. Despite this, I think it *is* appropriate to our present purposes to try and summarize what the report has to say on this issue even though space will limit the use of direct quotation to a minimum.

Having started with a review of the legal and historical background to the present situation, the report then notes that although majority opinion in the schools seems to favour 'the continued provision of some form of regular school worship', 'the desirability of a daily act of corporate worship continuing to be a statutory obligation on all types of primary and secondary schools' was subject to widespread questioning. This distinction between 'school worship as such' and 'the existing statutory requirements' governing the provision of worship is, however, not the only distinction which has to be made. The report detects a confusion in many people's thinking between 'school assembly' and 'school worship'.

> These are not synonymous, they have only become so through use and custom. It would be quite possible for the school assembly to be a wholly secular ceremony, somewhat akin to the 'opening exercises' in the schools of the USA. Such a ceremony could be an expression of the school's corporate life, an agency for transmitting ideals, and a valuable mood-setting formality. It could provide a forum for the giving of notices and exhortations by the head teacher. But this would not be an act of worship (§ 294).

The report then concentrates on the issue of 'school worship as such'. The point is made that 'an act of worship has two main elements: the expressive and the didactic'. The operation of the didactic element is to be seen in the fact that 'through joining in the ritual, the participant is instructed by

85

readings, by the words of hymns and psalms, by addresses, and to some extent by symbolic acts and movements' (§ 300). The role of this didactic element in school worship, it is claimed, will be of equal importance for all pupils, whatever their own beliefs, being part of the religious *education* provided by the school. If we take 'the exploration of the place and significance of religion in human life' as the basic function of RE, then this process *must* include 'some exploration of the meaning of worship'. 'The exploration of religious beliefs through classroom study and discussion requires to be complemented by that exploration of religious practice which the experience of worship provides' (§ 297).

When we turn to the *expressive* element, however, we appear to be up against a major problem, the problem noted by the Plowden Report, the problem of 'mixed religious or non-religious backgrounds'. The Durham Report tackles the problem as follows. It first tries to define the expressive element in worship in more precise terms. It notes that the traditional purpose of Christian worship could be defined as being 'to respond appropriately to the love and grace of God as seen in Jesus Christ, and to make the divine power a reality in the lives of the worshippers'. It is suggested that during occasions of school worship staff and pupils who are 'practising Christians' (or who are 'from practising Christian homes') will be able to express their response to God in this sort of way, be it an expression of adoration, penitence, thanksgiving, petition, dedication or whatever. However, to confine one's understanding of the expressive element in worship to these specifically Christian (or perhaps theistic) responses 'is to adopt too restrictive a definition'.

It is our view that an act of worship cannot solely be defined as a religious ritual whereby believers respond to the God in whom they believe. For one person, attendance at an act of worship may be expressive of deep religious faith; for another, it may be an expression of humility and awe before the mystery of Being; for another it may be only an expression of world-weariness and fear, of a desire to rest in the eternal

86

changelessness. Attendance at an act of worship does not necessarily imply or presuppose total personal commitment to the object of worship. . . . For some it will be an expression of faith; for others it will be an expression of a desire for faith; for others all that may be expressed is interest, desire for expansion of experience, and an awareness of the religious quest (§ 296, 299).

At this point the report is able to turn once again to the question of school *assembly*, and ask whether the understanding of worship set out in the previous paragraphs throws new light on the possible place of worship within the school assembly. It recognizes that

many schools will wish to have some assemblies at which worship does not take place. On these occasions there may be addresses on matters of public concern by the head teacher, or a member of staff, or a visiting speaker. Or there may be selections from great music and literature. We recognize the educational value of assemblies of this kind [6] (§ 312).

But of course the crucial word in this paragraph is 'some' – *some* assemblies, not all, should have this character. There should also be other, regular occasions of assembly, the report argues, which consist quite definitely of acts of worship. The reasons for this are two-fold. One is that, as we have seen, 'the experience of worship is a necessary part of religious education' and the most satisfactory way of providing this experience is by linking it with the school assembly. The other reason is that, as we have also seen, 'school assembly is an educationally and culturally significant event, expressive of society's values and (when properly conducted) influential in the creation of the atmosphere of the school community' (§ 307).

Notice that the phrase here is 'expressive of *society's* values'. The report had already rejected the suggestion that school assembly should consist of 'some form of ceremony expressing shared values within each individual school community, as interpreted by the staff and pupils'. It was felt that 'to hand over the problem to the individual schools would be an evasion of the issue. ... The nature of the school's community act is a matter of public concern and one which has public significance' (§ 305).

By setting the issue against this wider background, the report obviously has to pursue the argument beyond the confines of the school:

> The question is therefore: What system of values does society wish to see respected and expressed in its publicly provided schools? But behind this lies another and more crucial question: What is the belief-system of the English people? For values and beliefs are essentially interconnected. We reject the view that England is a post-Christian, religiously neutral society. We believe it to be more accurate to describe England as a post-ecclesiastical society, evincing varying degrees of Christian commitment and association. It is certainly quite false to describe present-day England as a secularist society, consciously and positively committed to a secular humanist interpretation of life. All the evidence presented to us, together with our own study and discussion of the question, leads us to the conclusion that, at present, society in England is positively rather than negatively disposed to religion and to an acceptance of Christian personal, spiritual, and moral values. We judge that society wishes to see these values respected and expressed in schools (§ 307).

Obviously, the report acknowledges, where schools are situated in areas where non-Christian religions predominate, then special provision will need to be made, but the general situation in the country at large suggests that 'the worship in most county schools will continue to be placed within the Christian tradition' (§ 313).

This is bound to raise in the minds of some (be they staff, pupils or parents) the question as to how far they can associate themselves with a corporate act which takes a specifically Christian form. The report would answer such conscientious scruples by pointing to its earlier comments about the wide open implications of 'attendance at an act of worship' (see

§ 296/9 quoted above). It makes the further comment on this point that worship at school assembly can be closely compared 'with those acts of worship for specific occasions which are a feature of our national life'.

> Events such as assize services, public memorial services, and days of remembrance are religious services in which the community comes before God in a corporate act. Such services do not presuppose the individual commitment of all those who attend them; they have a symbolic significance, representing society's disposition towards religion. They also meet society's ritual needs (§ 302).

A parallel must be drawn here with the report's argument for the continuing predominance of Christian material as a starting point in religious education work in the classroom (see pp. 51–2 above). That argument was not based on any claim that Christianity is *true*, but on the fact that it is the religious system most familiar to the majority of the pupils. Similarly here, the argument is not that the schools should reflect Christian values in their communal ritual acts because these are the only justifiable values to hold, but because they are the values most widely held throughout the country.

A similar argument was applied at an even more fundamental level in an earlier chapter in the report where consideration was being given to the 'model of man' underlying our educational structures.

> If we choose not to accept the Christian concept of man then two further alternatives meet us: either we accept some other model, or we consciously refuse to accept any model at all (§ 136).

Candidature for acceptance as 'the other model' might well be found in Marxist or behaviourist circles, to name but two, but (the report asks) are these any more universally acceptable than the Christian model? Clearly not.

> There remains, then, the possibility of leaving the matter open. . . . In theory this is a position of considerable attractiveness.

89

That the secular State should not adopt a standpoint appears to be open, liberal, and tolerant. In practice, however, it is open to at least as many objections as the alternative of choosing a model. From the standpoint of person or state, neutrality is virtually unachievable. In every educational discipline to do with man, evaluative elements appear which are often the more insidious for being unexamined (§ 137).

This is the real ground on which the Durham Report builds its case. It says, in effect, let us not pretend that our educational communities have no evaluative presuppositions; let us strive to agree on a form in which these underlying values may be acceptably expressed and openly explored; while acknowledging that some may wish to withhold personal commitment to this particular form, the Christian 'vehicles of vision' still provide the most widely acceptable frame of symbolic and ritual expression for the country as a whole and so for the country's schools in particular.

However, one should not ignore the fact that the report did make the definite recommendation that within this basically Christian frame some room should be found for 'assemblies at which worship does not take place', but which would 'transmit ideals' through the use, say, of selections from great music and literature. This idea was developed a little in the brief account of a seminar organized by the Department of Education and Science in 1969, published under the title *Religious Education: Present and Future*. At first sight it looks as if the schools referred to in the paper have adopted the third of the Durham Report's 'three positions', the position of neutrality:

Some schools have already demonstrated that it is possible to design assemblies which appear useful and credible to humanist and secular staff and pupils as well as to Christians. In such schools the assembly is not always religious (in the narrow sense) in tone and content; over a period it provides an exchange of philosophies and approaches to life, and the Christian and the humanist alike add to their knowledge of each other's beliefs and practices. Such a spirit of dialogue can greatly enrich a school.[7]

This suggestion that the function of school assembly is to promote 'dialogue' is an extremely interesting one. It appears to give due recognition to the fact that society (both society in its widest, national sense, and society as represented in the microcosm of the school) does not have one common mind on certain fundamental issues. It also seems to be more consistent with the whole concept of religious education as being an open-ended process. Not only is it 'open' in the classroom, but it is 'open' in assembly.

But how far is such a situation fully open? How far would a school, by adopting this pattern of assembly, be committing itself in fact to a neutral position? To what level of pre-supposition, if one can use that phrase, would this neutrality penetrate? If a school is taking an apparent position of neutrality between humanism and Christianity in its assemblies, is it thereby committing itself to a neutral position regarding the 'model of man' which underlies its whole educational enterprise? As we have already seen, acceptance of the possibility of open-ended, exploratory religious education 'is a consequence of the Christian's particular attitude to the world, and may not necessarily characterize that of any other faith' (Durham Report, §113). Would 'dialogue' be possible if the school's underlying assumptions were clearly Marxist ones? Theoretical considerations suggest it would not be, and experience confirms this.

So we see that even a school which looks on its assemblies as means whereby it explores its own presuppositions and values, is at one and the same time affirming thereby a definite set of basic presuppositions and values. Whether these merit the description 'Christian' or 'humanist' depends on how one interprets these two terms in the first place. (At all events they are not 'secularist' presuppositions, inasmuch as the secularist would assert that no value at all could be found in a theistic account of things, and therefore 'dialogue with Christianity' could serve no educational purpose whatsoever.) In many ways it does not matter which precise label is used, so long as it is a label which does not preclude open exploration.

However, there will still be occasions when a school will have to decide (and, as we have seen, for all practical purposes this will mean that the head will have to decide) whether a specifically Christian ceremony is appropriate or not (say, at an assembly to mark the beginning of a new school year). Perhaps this decision is seen at its sharpest if one asks whether prayer, in any form, should be included in the ceremony or not. Obviously to exclude prayer, and to use material which is equally acceptable to theists and non-theists alike, is to identify the occasion as a humanist rather than a Christian one; it is not to adopt a neutral position. The compromise has often been suggested of using silence, during which (as the well-worn Dean Inge anecdote puts it) 'Christians may pray and free-thinkers may think freely'. This may, in certain circumstances, be a compromise which has to be adopted, though it is not one which could be used if *specific* prayers were desired. Nor, of course, is 'shared silence' an answer to the problem of prayer in hymn-form (though in some boys' school assemblies it may often feel as if this were the solution being attempted despite all the exertions of the accompanying pianist!). If prayer in any form is used, then, this marks the ceremony out as at least a theistic one. How far, we must ask again, is a headteacher being consistent with the principles of open RE if he arranges a specifically Christian ceremony to mark some special occasion in the life of the school?

This issue, as I see it, is entirely analogous to the issue of the head's responsibility in the moral field. In the classroom, in discussion, moral enquiry must be left entirely open-ended, all viewpoints must be given due hearing. In practice, however, in the life of the school, certain patterns of behaviour will be commended and encouraged, others will be firmly ruled out. Similarly, open-ended RE in the classroom is quite compatible with 'the communication of a definite position' on certain significant occasions in school assemblies, and this not simply when it might be seen as exemplifying 'what certain people believe', but when it is clearly intended to be expressive of the school's own underlying values, and indeed a reflection of the underlying values of society itself.

The whole burden of the argument of this chapter has been that there is no such thing as a completely open approach this side of intellectual anarchy. As part of the process of establishing the constraints within which freedom and openness have to operate a school is justified in commending certain values, standards and presuppositions to its pupils. Note that the term is 'commend to' rather than 'demand of', and note also that the school's commendation will have to be fully open to challenge and discussion by the pupils in the classroom, a point which must be acknowledged and accepted by the whole community.[8] This would seem to me to constitute as fully open an approach as is consistent with an enterprise which is truly educational.

NOTES

1. Dearden, *op. cit.*, pp. 59f.

2. C. J. Macy (ed.), *Let's Teach Them Right*, Pemberton 1969.

3. See Derek Wright, *The Psychology of Moral Behaviour*, Penguin Books 1971, pp. 177–81.

4. *Humanities for the Young School Leaver: An Approach through Religious Education*, Evans/Methuen 1969, p. 52.

5. See Colin Alves, *Religion and the Secondary School*, SCM Press 1968, p. 20, § 12.

6. It should be noted that the Durham Report does not give any support to the idea of purely administrative assemblies whose sole function is to enable notices to be given out. When one bears in mind the large numbers of pupils so often involved, and the long distances between classroom and hall, then 'calling an assembly' simply as a method of communicating information would seem to be very wasteful of time and effort.

7. *Report on Education, No. 58*, HMSO, September 1969. This passage is also quoted in Schools Council Working Paper 36, pp. 98f. For still further development of these ideas see John Hull, 'Worship and the curriculum', *Journal of Curriculum Studies*, *1*, November 1969, pp. 208–19.

8. Cf. Alves, *op. cit.*, p. 186.

5 The Church in Education

A footnote to paragraph 510 of the Durham Report suggests that one very pragmatic reason why the churches should continue to maintain their own system of day schools in this country is that there is 'a potential possibility', even if not 'a foreseeable possibility', that RE might drop out of the county school curriculum 'either by default or by deliberate decision' (the latter reflecting a definite shift in society's underlying values).

Some Christians might feel that that moment has virtually arrived already. Their interpretation of the present situation is that Christianity has been forced out of the schools. They would point to the fact that twenty, even ten, years ago most schools accepted the requirements of the 1944 Education Act and quite willingly put them into effect. Morning assembly was indeed conceived of in the terms used by the Newsom Report – 'a time in which pupils and teachers seek help in prayer and pause to recollect the presence of God'. RE was a process fully governed by Agreed Syllabuses which were compiled by bodies on which the church had fifty per cent representation by right, and the purpose of these syllabuses was often couched in phrases such as those used in the Introduction to the 1949 revision of the Cambridgeshire Syllabus:

> To teach Christianity to our children is to inspire them with the vision of the glory of God in the face of Jesus Christ, and to send them into the world willing to follow him (p. 9).

Nowadays, in contrast, they would claim, morning assembly

(if in fact it is held at all) is thought of either as an administrative convenience, or at most an occasion of 'dialogue', designed to 'appear useful and credible to humanist and secular staff'. And RE has been forced to abandon any procedures or purposes which might be labelled 'indoctrinatory', and as a result has been reduced to a vague exchanging of unchallenged opinion on matters of mainly ethical concern, or a purely academic study of the practices and doctrines of 'world religions' where Christianity only gets a brief look-in if it is lucky. The idea of 'teaching for commitment' is of course quite out, being an affront to the sacred principle of pupil autonomy. Therefore, the argument goes, Christians should stop wasting their time working within a system where all the cards are stacked against them, and concentrate instead on making church schools more effectively places where *real* Christian education can be provided.

There will be no need for me to say how wrong I think this argument to be. It would seem to me to be based on two misconceptions: (1) a misrepresentation of the present position in the county schools; (2) a misunderstanding of the function of church schools. Let us examine these misconceptions in turn.

As I have tried to show in the previous three chapters, the general stress on 'autonomy' in educational thinking and the openness of the present situation in RE *derives from* a concept of man which is basic to Christian thought. The new developments are therefore not antagonistic to a Christian understanding of the educational process, nor opposed to a continuing Christian presence within education in this country. I know that the most dangerously false prophets are those who cry 'peace' when there is no peace, and I recognize that there is 'a potential possibility' that the educational enterprise in this country may break loose from the Christian roots which have so far fed and informed its growth. But I firmly believe that that time has not yet come.

The two most obvious moves which might seem to indicate such a fundamental change in character within the country's schools would be the abolition of RE and the total disappearance of Christian forms of assembly. These are not the only possible indicators of a fundamental change of direction. There could be administrative and disciplinary changes which either capitulated to the wildest demands for the removal of all restraints on freedom, or else reacted strongly against those demands by imposing heavily authoritarian structures. (Indeed this latter reaction could appear to be strengthening RE and assembly by incorporating them into these structures, whereas in fact, of course, the Christian presuppositions basically underlying the whole process would themselves have been swept aside.) Or there could be curricular changes which denied the concept of 'all-round' education, or at least acted on the theory that the only concern of the *schools* was the development of basic skills and therefore deliberately ignored the cultural and personal aspects of development. Or again there could be curricular and administrative changes which reflected a belief that the schools were simply agents of national prosperity and therefore should concentrate on the maximum development of applied intelligence and vocational skills, firmly coupled with the fostering of a sense of national loyalty (and again forms of RE and assembly could be used in this sort of operation). Nevertheless it is still true that a more insidious shift of emphasis, signifying a possibly unconscious drifting away from Christian presuppositions and values, may well be heralded by a loss of concern for RE and the *ceremony* of assembly.

As we have already remarked, there may well be some observers of the current scene (both from within the educational world and from outside it) who would claim to see precisely such a loss of concern already creeping up on us. Particularly would they point to the wide interest in the process of 'integrating' the timetable, either totally (as in some primary schools) or in certain areas such as 'Humanities' or 'Social Studies' (as in some secondary schools). In these circumstances RE as such disappears from the timetable, and becomes 'an element within' whatever integrated pattern is adopted.

The Durham Report was somewhat cautious in its reaction to these developments:

> Educationally considered, the inclusion of religious education in integrated studies has much to commend it. The ways in which religion affects our daily lives, or how beliefs about the nature of the world affect behaviour in it, are more readily appreciated when the tendency towards fragmentation of knowledge has been resisted and when the pupil is allowed to perceive something of its unity. . . . Yet over against this we have to recognize that the Christian faith has a distinctive body of biblical and doctrinal teaching which has to be understood in its own terms as well as being studied in its inter-disciplinary relatedness (§ 256, 255).

The Schools Council Working Paper 36 gives very much more attention to the question (eight pages, as opposed to five paragraphs) but even so emerges with a similarly cautious conclusion, being content to leave the reader with a list of (very apposite) questions to be borne in mind, and a reference to the earlier Schools Council publication, *Humanities for the Young School Leaver: An Approach through Religious Education*,[1] which had of course been concerned solely with the problems and possibilities of the integrated situation. This earlier document was basically an account of some experimental work done with groups of school leavers, prefaced by a theoretical consideration of the rationale of 'integrating' RE with other subjects, and followed by an appraisal of the failures and successes of the experiment.

> The final and most obstinate problem encountered in our experimental courses was the problem of arriving at a point where religious propositions were seen to be relevant (p. 31).

However, (and this is the crucial point) this was felt to be fundamentally a *methodological* problem, not one which was insoluble by the very nature of the situation. Indeed the nature of the situation virtually demands that religion

D

should find its place within the framework of an integrated programme:

> Religion is not an optional extra in the interpretation of human life, nor a last expedient in meeting the demands of life when all else fails. It is, rather, a dimension of all experience. It is the full understanding of the whole of life – life viewed *sub specie aeternitatis*. It follows that any problem, if pushed far enough, becomes a religious problem. To single out some problems as more 'religious' than others is to betray a misunderstanding of the meaning of religion (p. 10).

What Christians must keep a careful watch on, therefore, is not the extent to which schools *attempt*, now and in the future, to bring RE within an integrated scheme, but the extent to which they fail to do this *effectively*.

The same is true with reference to new approaches to assembly. Some schools are experimenting with sectional assemblies (house assemblies, form prayers, etc.), while others are examining the consequences of holding assembly at less frequent intervals than in the past. In some cases this may indeed be motivated by a desire on the part of the head-teacher to be freed from the whole range of responsibility which is implied in the concept of assembly (for responsibility it *is*), and Christians should certainly be on the look-out for any attempt to repudiate this responsibility in any official or permanent way. On the other hand, the fact that experiments to discover more *effective* forms of assembly are taking place should be a cause for satisfaction, not alarm, however unconventional some of those experiments may be.

In any case, as I indicated above, what Christians really need to be sensitive to is the extent to which there is continuing acceptance of the Christian 'concept of man' as forming the groundwork of all our educational endeavours. Only if the Christian churches were convinced that this had been finally abandoned in our national educational system would they be justified in calling for retrenchment within the walls of our existing church schools.

But are church schools in any case places which would lend themselves to such an act of retrenchment? Can they be 'places where *real* Christian education is provided'? Of course the answer to these questions depends on what 'real Christian education' is assumed to be. But there is the further question of whether church schools, as now conceived, do (or should) carry the ghetto-like function which this hypothetical future development would demand of them. Clearly we must now look at the whole concept of the church school and see what sort of institution it is.

Of course the truth of the matter is that there is not one concept of the church school, but many. When the Durham Commission came to examine the position of Church of England schools, they had to start by making a distinction between the church's concern for the education of all men and its concern for the education of its own community in particular. (These two aspects of its concern the report labelled as 'general' and 'domestic' respectively.) Then there is the further distinction which has sometimes been made between 'secular' education and 'religious' education. Within its own domestic community the church has been concerned to provide both secular and religious education, for the simple reason that originally there were no other schools from which secular education could be obtained, had the church schools concentrated solely on the religious aspects of education.

Today the Roman Catholic church schools (or Roman Catholic voluntary schools, to give them their official title) maintain this two-fold domestic function, the religious-cum-secular education of the Roman Catholic community's own children. 'Every Catholic child from a Catholic home to be taught by Catholic teachers in a Catholic school' has been the ideal which the Roman Catholic Church has traditionally set itself in this country. Within the Church of England, however, a quite different concept has developed. For a very long time, as far as the Church of England was concerned, the distinction between 'general' and 'domestic' concerns was hardly apparent, 'for nation and church were, theoretically, one'. As a result, even when at last in 1870 a complementary system of schools was set up throughout the country for which the church was not financially responsible, people nevertheless felt that a large measure of responsibility was still laid upon the church, and that it should be contributing as much as possible to the general education of the nation as well as to that of its own domestic community (which was beginning to emerge as a partially distinguishable body – but only *partially* distinguishable – within the community at large).

When the Durham Commission eventually made their recommendations concerning the future of Church of England voluntary schools, they had this historical background to the present position very much in mind. Their recommendation was that, despite the continuing financial burden this would involve, the church should continue to maintain some system of voluntary schools, though (unlike the Roman Catholic approach) this should *not* be for primarily 'domestic' reasons. The two primary reasons the report did give for this recommendation were:

> (a) church schools are important as providing a means whereby the church's general presence in education may be realized;
> (b) individual church schools are important because they possess certain educational potentialities not necessarily found in schools of other kinds (§ 519).

In comment on the first of these points the report said, among other things:

> If the church ceases to be directly involved in the work of education, it will cease to be involved with modern society at one of its most creative points, where the church can both hope to contribute to the development of society and can learn from society (*ibid.*).

The dual crux of this argument is that the church cannot experience the necessary 'direct involvement' in education

100

simply through the involvement of 'individual teachers, advisers, committee members, administrators', etc., within the state system, even though the church's involvement does indeed operate through such people. Equally it will not be 'involved with society' in this vital field if it restricts its educational activity to the purely domestic task of educating the members of its own community. Therefore it must continue to maintain schools of its own, but it must also throw these schools open to all children 'whose homes are in the natural area served by the school' (§ 527) and not restrict entry to the families of regular members of the local church congregation.

But this is not to ignore the second complementary justification of the voluntary school. Not only is it for the good of the church that such schools should exist; it is for the good of the school community as well. Assuming that the voluntary school is not inappropriately situated (that it is not, for example, right in the middle of a solidly Muslim immigrant community) then there is a reasonable chance that 'a church school can become an educational community which brings into explicit focus the shared assumptions of parents and teachers' (§ 520). As the report recognizes, a number of county schools have been able to become precisely such communities, nevertheless 'the church school is in a particularly advantageous position in this respect'.

> Where a stable context for personal development is provided by a healthy consonance of school and home, each in its turn related to a church which is itself a positive source of influence in the local community, then the educational processes operating in that situation receive an extra dimension (§ 484).

The report acknowledges the need to maintain a careful balance here between keeping the school open to virtually all comers and yet producing a school community which is able to take certain assumptions for granted, assumptions which are 'exemplified by the link with the church'. On the latter score it is expected that in a church school ' "religious" assemblies might be more frequent than in a county school' if future developments are as predicted (§ 524); that the local incumbent will make it his concern to develop 'effective contact between the life of the school and the life of the local congregation' (§ 530); and that in the RE done in the school, 'through its links with the local congregations and the local clergy its pupils will be able to feel something of what it means to belong to a worldwide Christian society' (§ 555). On the other hand, the report is very careful to point out that the *aim* of RE, even in a church school of this sort, should still be open-ended. The suggestion that 'the church's real interest in maintaining its schools is because they provide fruitful recruiting grounds' is strongly repudiated (§ 521).

To emphasize this point the report makes two recommendations concerning the church school of the future, namely that 'instruction in the catechism as part of preparation for confirmation' should no longer be thought of as part of the school curriculum (as it has regularly been in many church schools in the past); and that all RE in church schools 'should be open to inspection by Her Majesty's Inspectors'. In the past, because it has been looked on 'as a purely denominational exercise', RE in church schools[2] has not been inspected as other subjects have been.

> But wherever religious education has the open, educationally defined aims which we have set forward, then it would be wrong to single it out from every other subject by not opening it to the general oversight of HMI (§ 557).

So the church school of the future, if the report's recommendations are carried out, would reflect much more the church's 'general' concern with education (which it has inherited from the past) rather than a specifically 'domestic' concern whose ideal would parallel that of the Roman Catholic Church in the past – 'every church child from a church home to be taught by church teachers in a church school'. And it would certainly be only on this latter basis

102

that the church schools could be used for the sort of ghetto-operation that was being advocated by the argument we were examining at the beginning of this chapter.

Retrenchment, then, is neither necessary at the moment, nor would it be appropriate unless the educational system in this country shifted its basis completely and repudiated all its past values. It would be a counsel of utter despair to suggest that Christian teachers should start preparing for the eventuality of such a situation by all coming together and retreating behind closed doors. Quite the opposite. We should ensure that the church's educational doors remain as wide open as possible, so that it can continue 'to be involved with society at one of its most creative points'.

In fact the Durham Report itself was strongly criticized for concentrating so much of its attention on the future of church schools, and failing to place enough emphasis on ways in which the church could be more fully involved in the state system.[3] To be completely fair, the report was not unaware of this possible source of criticism. It had noted as one of the objections to the very existence of church schools that the fact that they are there can cause 'an unhappy limitation of the Christian concern of the church so that it concentrates too much of its attention and resources on the schools of its own denomination and shows too little concern for the religious education of children in county schools' (p. 200, note 1); or again, 'the church school, by virtue of remaining identifiably different, may act as a distorting magnet within the educational system, attracting to itself the service of Christian teachers who should be spread abroad throughout the system as a whole' (§ 467).

There is obviously a great deal of truth in this charge, particularly in the first of these two versions of the objection. It is not only in the realm of education that the church has far too often been concerned with domestic matters at the expense of its involvement in matters of more general import. However, there is an equal danger in the opposite extreme. Were the church to become completely involved in

103

general concerns and operate exclusively in secular situations, it could soon lose all sense of its distinct corporate identity. As I have suggested elsewhere[4] the widely current symbol of the church as servant may provide a useful corrective to the more magisterial and imperialistic symbols from the past, but it would be absurd to suggest that the church is here simply to do what society requires of it. An equally important, and equally biblical, symbol is to be found in the image of salt, whose functions were (in the days before disinfectants and refrigerators) to cleanse and to preserve in a healthy state. (Unfortunately this reference of the symbol has often been ignored, and attention has been diverted to salt's capacity to add flavour. In this light the function of the church in relation to the world would seem to be analogous to the effect of tomato ketchup on a fishcake.)

The church must therefore ensure that, whatever form her educational involvement may take, the result of this involvement, for the world, will be an improvement in the quality and soundness of the educational process as a whole. Unfortunately this result has not always been achieved. It has been only rarely that the church has managed to concentrate sufficient attention and energy to make any distinctive impact on the world of education. Obviously in the years leading up to the 1944 Education Act, a great deal of effort was brought to bear on the whole question of the future development of education in this country, and the church clearly exerted considerable influence on the pattern of development which was then established. But subsequently the church seems to have given its attention, in practical terms, almost solely to its own domestic educational scene.

There have, of course, been notable exceptions to this. The Roman Catholic catechetical centres have been of enormous value to RE teachers in all types of school. The work of Anglican Diocesan Advisers has developed in some areas so that their concern is now with county as well as voluntary schools. In Bristol, for example, this has been taken to the point where a joint appointment between Diocese and LEA has been made. But even in these instances the church seems to be concerned almost entirely with the *religious* education in the county schools. Not very much concerted, or official, effort has gone into attempting to influence the quality of *overall* education in the state system. Individual members of the church may well be exerting most effective influence in this direction in isolated pockets, but the church as a whole, either at diocesan or central level, has done very little in this direction in the twenty-five years since the 1944 Education Act, either in terms of practical action or in terms of policy assessment. This is true both of the denominational and the ecumenical scene. 'The church's voice' is heard speaking frequently in some form or another on matters of international affairs and social responsibility, but on broad educational matters the church appears to remain silent. The only public manifestation of the church's concern with education (apart from specifically religious education) in recent years has been the report[5] of the Methodist Conference Commission on Education which attempted to state 'a reasoned Christian view of the place of education in the community'. (I must stress that the above paragraph refers only to what has been happening (or, rather, *not* happening) in this country. Work done by the WCC/WCCE Joint Study Commission on Education has opened up a large number of these general issues, as its report presented at the Uppsala Assembly showed.)

Admittedly the Church of England has recently embarked on a reorganization of its central educational committee structure in the hope that this will enable the General Synod's Board of Education more fully to carry out its official responsibility for 'the formulation of the overall policy of the Church of England in the field of education and for its co-operation with the State'. What is more, the even more recent report[6] of the Carlisle Commission on the purpose and function of the educational machinery at diocesan level also asserts that the church should be deeply, and practically, concerned with the general educational system:

105

We deprecate the notion that the church's concern for education is to be identified with, or even largely directed towards, the maintenance of church schools. Disproportionate attention to their affairs involves the relative neglect of areas with which the church should be seriously and urgently engaged (§ 56).

Of course the report goes on to make the further assertion that

wider engagement implies no diminution of the importance of church schools; on the contrary, their significance is enhanced if they are seen as a living and visible expression of the church's genuine care for all education (*ibid.*).

These words would find a ready echo in many other pronouncements on church schools and they come very near to one of the arguments employed in the Durham Report (see above, on p. 100, where § 519 is quoted). However, one must be careful how one interprets the phrase 'seen as a living and visible expression'. Later in its chapter on church schools the Carlisle Report notes (NB *notes*, not necessarily approves) various arguments which have been put forward in their defence. One of these is phrased as follows:

The Christian doctrine of man is of cardinal importance for education; the church schools should exemplify – and are in a position specially to exemplify – that significance and its practical application for living.

A later argument in the same list appears in these words:

If the church, as part of its service to the community, claims to offer a contribution to thinking about education, it is better fitted to do so if it is engaged in that enterprise, sharing both its achievements and frustrations and bearing some of the attendant responsibilities (§ 76, points *a* and *h*).

There is both common ground but also significant differences of detail in these two positions (the second of which is the form represented in the Durham Report). Both imply that because the church holds a distinctive doctrine of man, it therefore has a deep concern with education in all its forms, and also has a clear duty to maintain its public witness to this concern. This witness (bearing in mind the symbol of the church as salt) may well involve the bringing to bear of a corrective influence on the educational world at large. The first formula sees the function of the church school in this task as being to provide the public stage on which the church may *exemplify* the implications of its beliefs.[7] The second formula, on the other hand, sees the church school as providing the point at which the church can be fully involved with education in all its aspects (administrative as well as pedagogical), thereby enabling the church to speak on educational matters 'with the only authority which will be heeded today, the authority which is derived from direct experience' (*The Fourth R*, § 519). The Durham Report in fact refrained from putting forward the idea of the church school as an 'exemplar', particularly in present circumstances, for two reasons. In the first place it recognized that under certain conditions county schools could achieve precisely the same quality of community as church schools, and secondly it acknowledged that church schools have by no means all created an 'exemplary' public image for themselves in the past.

Everyone will be aware, from their own experience, of church schools which have in the past fallen well short of the standards of their neighbouring county schools. This may be for perfectly understandable reasons, shortage of finance for necessary development being paramount among these. On the other hand it must be admitted that it is the 'special' nature of church schools which has given rise in some instances to special abuses which could, and should, have been avoided. There have been cases where, simply to show its independence of the LEA, church schools have deliberately clung to outdated methods and approaches when all other schools in the area have taken advantage of innovatory procedures. (There have equally, and equally regrettably, been cases where the LEAs have failed to extend full supporting facilities to church schools to enable them to keep pace with 'their own' schools.) Even more regrettably there have been cases where the right of parents to send their children to a church school rather than a county school (where they exist in close enough proximity) has enabled church schools to be chosen for quite reprehensible reasons. This has led to some church schools being turned virtually into free prep. schools, because parental choice has been exercised (and allowed to be exercised, what is more) largely according to the dividing lines of social class. Others, even more reprehensibly, have been turned into white enclaves in predominantly coloured areas. These disturbing developments obviously could not possibly be described as 'exemplary' in either sense of that word. They neither 'exemplify' the significance of the Christian doctrine of man, nor could they be pointed to as good 'examples' for other schools to follow. However, they could be seen as an instance of 'the frustrations of the educational enterprise', part of that 'direct experience' from which the church is able to learn (if it is willing to face up to its own failures) and so is able to contribute from within to the educational debates of the community at large.

But, some might say, what about the work of the church school in *religious* education? Can it not be an 'exemplar' there? This is of course to bring the discussion back once again to the narrower confines we were trying to break out of earlier in the chapter. But there is here the further problem we have already touched on, the problem of the *aims* of religious education in a church school. We have seen that the Durham Report suggested that there should be no distinction between the aims of the subject in a church school and the aims of the subject in a county school. The differences, such as they were, would be concerned with methods.[8] Now this may have been the recommendation of the Durham Report, but does it in fact represent the situation in the actual church schools, now or in the foreseeable future? It

108

is surely only if the aims of the subject in the two kinds of school *are* the same that the church school could hope to be an 'exemplar' for the county schools.

The church must clearly make up its mind on this issue. It is typical of its present uncertainty that the Carlisle Report should have commended the job specification suggested for diocesan RE advisers by the (now defunct) Church of England Children's Council. This document clearly linked work in church schools with work in the 'voluntary' field (i.e. Sunday schools and the like). This would suggest that there is at least a possibility of the purpose of the church's educational activity in both these fields being the same. In the past the Sunday school has usually been looked on as having definitely 'initiatory' aims, and many have assumed that this is the purpose of the church day school as well. It was no fictitious parish which said 'We have a church day school. What do we need a Sunday school for as well?' And certainly as far as Roman Catholic day schools are concerned there has been little doubt that one of the main purposes of the school should be the 'formation' of the pupils as practising, believing Christians; there would be little support here (officially, at least) for the thesis that 'the teacher should not measure the success of his teaching by the extent to which his pupils agree with him'.[9]

Yet, as well as commending the Children's Council document, the Carlisle Report follows the Durham Report in recommending that RE in church schools should be open to inspection by HMI (p. 129), thereby suggesting the opposite view that the aims of RE in church schools is not the same as in Sunday school, but the same as in any county school. It admits its own uncertainty on the issue.

> We make this suggestion conscious of the problem which, so far as we can discover, has not been thoroughly investigated as it ought to be, i.e. what *educationally* is the difference between religious education in the 'Sunday school' and religious education in the day school (§ 222).

The Durham Report had of course insisted that a 'closed type' of RE was 'quite indefensible in the day school'. And what it meant by 'a closed type' was

> a purely domestic type of denominational instruction which starts with the assumption that all the pupils are committed members of the Church of England and which has as its sole purpose the strengthening of that commitment' (§ 554).

The report then went on to suggest (though it did *not* 'thoroughly investigate the problem') that this 'closed type' of RE might not be 'defensible even in a Sunday school context'.

I am not suggesting that the problem can be given 'a thorough investigation' here either, but it is one which merits a certain amount of consideration in the present discussion, however brief. We are, of course, thrust here right into the heart of the indoctrination controversy. In his discussion of this issue R. F. Dearden distinguishes two aspects of indoctrination to which the educator must object. The first concerns the content of material taught, the second the aim with which it is taught. Antony Flew's definition of the former is 'the teaching of reasonably disputatious doctrines as if they were known facts'.[10] A definition of the latter is referred to by Dearden as 'getting people to believe things in such a way that nothing, not even good counter arguments, will shake those beliefs'.[11]

It obviously needs to be said at the very outset that no Christian teacher ought to be doing, or even attempting to do, either of these things. We have noted on a number of occasions the absolute necessity of distinguishing between different categories of understanding, of recognizing when it is appropriate to talk of 'knowledge', when of 'insight', when of 'conviction', etc. As to the second aspect, the indoctrinatory aim defined above so clearly invites brainwashing as the appropriate method for its fulfilment that no Christian could possibly contemplate such an approach to teaching. Admittedly phrases have been used which might at first seem

110

parallel to this objectionable definition. As we have seen, the Plowden Report contained the sentence, 'Children should not be confused by being taught to doubt before faith is established' (§ 572). But the whole context in which this perhaps unfortunately phrased comment came shows that nothing coming anywhere near the concept of brainwashing was in the minds of the committee, at any point of their argument.

And yet, despite all these necessary disclaimers, one can see what it was that led the Plowden Committee to speak in such terms, and one can see why many Sunday school teachers and clergy would feel perfectly justified in having as their aim 'the strengthening of their pupils' commitment'. In the first place, a great deal of what we acquire by way of presupposition comes to us by a process of absorption, through the growth of 'shared beliefs, values and attitudes'.[12] We *catch* an enthusiasm, we *respond to* an ideal. We are not taught these things in the way that we are taught facts or skills. But we do still need a channel of communication through which we can become aware of the beliefs, values and attitudes we may eventually come to share. They do not arise spontaneously within us. The two major channels which convey these intangibles are firstly appropriate language or some other form of symbolization; and secondly personal relationships, either between individuals or as expressed in community life.

With reference to the first of these channels the Carlisle Report speaks of Christian theology and the activity of specifically Christian teaching in these terms:

> The theology arising from such a revelation is a summons, urgent but not coercive, to see more and see it more profoundly, to know more and know it better, to love more and love more richly. It is to realize that the truth is a life into which we grow. Appropriate Christian speech about this kind of revelation is a matter of talking, and doing, in such a way that others find that they come of themselves to see what we see (§ 147).

Significantly this passage comes in the chapter on *adult* education. It implies a sophisticated awareness, in the minds of both teachers and taught, of the status of the language used in conveying this 'summons'. Such sophistication is obviously more than one can expect to find in young children, and so theological language tends to be used in Sunday schools, etc. as if it were literal, factual language. ('Used' by the teachers as well as 'understood' by the children in this way.) Hence the charge of indoctrination (in the first sense of the term) brought by the church's critics.

All that can be said about this problem in the space that is available to us is to stress that every Christian teacher, in whatever field he or she operates, must be aware of the status of the language which he uses, and must further recognize that when he is verbally communicating 'beliefs' to the children they will accept his statements by virtue of the authority which their *trust* in him has conferred; and this is all right. It is *not* all right if he exceeds the terms of that trust by claiming the authority of 'an exponent of proven certainties'. Nor must he attempt to build up such a sense of blind trust in him that his authority will never be questioned. He must be prepared as soon as the situation is ready for it to point to the fact that 'other trustworthy persons have different beliefs'.[13]

This obviously brings us to the second channel of communication, personal relationships and community life. Here there is no initial barrier to an appropriate response in the undeveloped child mind. The young members of a community can share in the fellowship of that community's life almost to the same extent as the adult members, can feel a sense of belonging which is just as deep as the adult's, and so in this way begin to absorb the 'shared beliefs, values and attitudes' which permeate the community. Once again, however, to avoid the charge of indoctrination (in its second aspect), one must not attempt to 'strengthen commitment' to the church to such an extent that it can do no wrong in the eyes of its members. As we saw in our earlier discussion of

Christian theology, the very nature of the Christian revelation demands 'the possibility of a built-in self-criticism' (*The Fourth R*, § 114). Hence for the growing pupil, even in the Sunday school situation, the ideal goal must eventually be a 'rational autonomy' of belief even within the supporting framework of the 'shared beliefs, values and attitudes' of the church's community life.

Recognition of the difficulties children have with theological language, coupled with their ease of entry into the sense of fellowship within the church has led to the suggestion that the immediate goal of Sunday school work should be simply the development of the children's sense of belonging (within the limits mentioned in the previous paragraph). This, of course, would force the church to look very seriously at the whole question of the education of its *adult* members. People would no longer be able to pretend to themselves that all children in the church had been 'taught the faith' in their Sunday school classes, and therefore there was no need for any educational activity at the adult level. It would be recognized, at last, that the appropriate level at which to 'teach the faith' is precisely the adult one.

But whether such a total shift of emphasis occurs or not, the church still needs to wake up to its responsibilities for the education of its adult members. As the Carlisle Report puts it:

> There is no such thing as a *finishing* school in the Christian concept of education. Education is never completed. The educated adult is to be detected in the extent to which he continues his own education, voluntarily, for the rest of his life (§ 146).

The church should be there to help him do just that, and in a whole variety of ways. It is disappointing that the banner which the Carlisle Report so vigorously waves should turn out only to have 'theology' emblazoned on it. Certainly it would be a very good thing if, as the report suggests, 'the university extra-mural departments and the WEA' would 'mount courses in theology and religious studies' as part of the church's adult education programme (§ 152), but there is much more to the matter than this. The report does itself indicate at one point the sort of thing that adult education should be:

> It is a genuine freeing of adults for responsible, informed, and articulate living in a world where the truth of the Christian religion is in question. Unbelief has come of age in prestige and confidence, and those who profess religious beliefs need to know how to live alongside educated and sensitive agnostics and atheists in love, honesty, and understanding. There must be no paternalistic peering over the ramparts of the bastions of belief but a genuine rapport with human beings who share the common oscillation between faith and doubt (§ 149).

There are some in the church who believe that this 'freeing' of people 'for responsible, informed and articulate living' can best be done by employing the insights of group and social psychology and exploring 'the problems of human relationships, of leadership and authority, of communication and organizational structure'. But this, too, is to misunderstand what is required. Such exploration may be a necessary part of the whole enterprise, more appropriate for some than for others, but what is needed throughout the church is some organization through which local, congregation-based groups can first of all become sufficiently informed, not primarily about their own psychological drives, nor primarily about recent developments in theology and religious studies, but about the world in which they live and the facts of the situation in which the contemporary church finds itself. They will then be in a position to discuss more effectively and more responsibly the problems confronting Christians both individually and collectively today, and through this discussion they can learn to identify and apply the insights that the Christian gospel brings with it. Programmes of this sort have appeared from time to time, and in one place or another, but a tremendous task remains to be done by way of gearing the whole church into a permanent enterprise of this sort.

In its chapter on church schools the Durham Report quoted two passages concerning the width and importance of the church's educational responsibilities. They bear repeating here.

> It is a Christian's concern for the wholeness of the human being, for the quality of the common life, for the direction in which man goes that turns him towards education now and sets him inside it and will not let him disengage.[14]

> We are in, and will remain in, education because that is where we belong. The pursuit of truth and the imparting of it are very much our business, as are the healthy enlargement of men's minds and personalities and the creation of truly human relationships and communities.[15]

I have tried to indicate in this chapter some of the different ways the Christian community in this country can be 'in' education. Perhaps for too long, in the past, the church was 'over' education. It has begun to learn its new relationship and its new role, and the consequences of all this for both its 'general' and its 'domestic' tasks, at all age levels. However, the new type of involvement has only just begun, and it is to be hoped that the church will quickly settle to the long and strenuous task which still lies ahead, and will not allow itself to be deflected by discouragement or disparagement from any source, external or internal.

NOTES

1. Published by Evans/Methuen, 1969. The discussion has been taken further in *Religious Education in Integrated Studies* ed. Ian H. Birnie, SCM Press 1972.

2. There has, of course, been a distinction on this matter between schools of *aided* status and schools of *controlled* status. In the latter the RE which is given 'according to the Agreed Syllabus' has always been open to inspection by HMI; the two periods a week of 'church teaching' which can by right be given has *not* been open to such inspection. In aided schools *no* RE has been open to inspection, as is indicated in the text of the chapter. For the sake

of simplicity I have not distinguished the different types of church school at any point in my résumé of the Durham Report's argument. The report itself, of course, goes into the varying situations in considerable detail.

3. See e.g. Dr Kathleen Bliss's comments on p. 17 of *Learning for Living*, September 1970 (SCM Press).

4. In the January 1970 edition of *Faith and Unity* (Church Union).

5. *Christian Commitment in Education*, Epworth Press 1970.

6. *Partners in Education*, National Society/SPCK 1971. The commission was set up in 1970 under the chairmanship of the Bishop of Carlisle and was sponsored by the National Society.

7. In a different section of its report (§ 71; cf. recommendation 27 on p. 128) the Carlisle Commission endorsed the view that the church school has an *exemplary* role, but it used the term more in the sense of being willing to pioneer new approaches rather than of attempting to offer perfected models of behaviour. This I would heartily endorse, though it must still be recognized that some approaches pioneered by a church school could not be taken up by a county school in the same form (work developing from a school celebration of the eucharist, for example).

8. There is also, of course, a further possible difference in the total context of presuppositions, the *ethos*, within the two types of school, but this, as we have argued above, is another issue altogether, not affecting the 'openness' of the RE work in the classroom.

9. *Humanities for the Young School Leaver: An Approach through Religious Education*, p. 11.

10. Antony Flew, in *Studies in Philosophy and Education*, vol. V, no. 2, p. 277. Quoted in an appendix to the Durham Report, 'Indoctrination' by Basil Mitchell.

11. See R. F. Dearden, *op. cit.*, p. 55. (The definition is derived from p. 181 of J. P. White's article on 'Indoctrination' in *The Concept of Education*, ed. R. S. Peters, Routledge & Kegan Paul 1967.)

12. See Basil Mitchell's article on 'Indoctrination', *The Fourth R*, p. 357.

13. See *Humanities for the Young School Leaver: An Approach through Religious Education*, pp. 51f.

14. From § 28 of the Report of the Joint Study Commission on Education, presented to the Fourth Assembly of the World

Council of Churches, Uppsala 1968. Quoted on p. 205 of the Durham Report.

15. From an article by the Rt Rev. A. J. Trillo, in *Looking Forward to the Seventies* ed. P. Bander, Colin Smythe 1968, p. 271. Quoted in § 438 of the Durham Report.

6 Wild Ecological Postscript

In the Foreword to this book I explained that one of my purposes in writing the book was to explain what lies behind recent developments in education in this country and particularly the changes occurring in RE. I have tried to look at some of the roots of change which can be discovered in the field of educational thinking itself, and at some which derive from new thinking about and in theology. Changes in both these fields make it imperative for the church to understand quite clearly what is happening in the schools, both generally and with specific reference to RE and assembly, for if it fails to understand it will forfeit its place within these educational developments and so lose contact with society in a vital area. This would, of course, do considerable damage to the effectiveness of the church's task in the world. It could also prove to be a disaster point in the developing story of the human race.

Without, at this point, wishing to make any special claims on behalf of the faith of the Christian church, I would nevertheless want to argue very strongly that the world is in desperate need of finding (or perhaps *re*-discovering) *some* faith. It is not only a matter of *individual* fulfilment that people today need to 'find a faith to live by'. It is a matter of world survival.

When I wrote *Religion and the Secondary School*[1] in 1967 I used as a closing quotation a passage from *The Phenomenon of Man* in which Teilhard was suggesting that man was passing through an age of transition.

What we are up against is the heavy swell of an unknown sea which we are just entering from behind the cape that protected us. At the cost of what we are enduring, life is taking a step, and a decisive step, in us and in our environment. After the long maturation that has been steadily going on during the apparent immobility of the agricultural centuries, the hour has come at last, characterised by the birth pangs inevitable in another change of state.[2]

Because of the difficulties that such a transition in social evolution involved, Teilhard was alarmed that mankind might not be prepared to accept what was demanded of it, might wish to escape by some means or other from the birth pangs and so would destroy not only its future but its present as well in the attempt.

Teilhard had, of course, written these words against the background of the Second World War, and by the early 1960s a new fluctuation of mood had occurred. Everyone was still very much aware of the *transitionary* nature of our present civilization. 'Change' was still very much a key concept in everyone's thinking. The Plowden Report's reaction to this was very typical of its day:

One obvious purpose of education is to fit children for the society into which they will grow up. To do this successfully it is necessary to predict what that society will be like. It will certainly be one marked by rapid and far reaching economic and social change (§ 494).

But it is not just that the Plowden Report noted the *fact* of change as being characteristic of our future. What is significant is what it anticipated the consequences of this change would be:

It is likely to be richer than now, with even more choice of goods, with tastes dominated by majorities and with more leisure for all (*ibid.*).

There were indeed certain dangers, spiritual dangers, which could be foreseen in such a future:

119

We fear that it will be much engrossed with the pursuit of material wealth, too hostile to minorities, too dominated by mass opinion and too uncertain of its values (§ 495).

These, however, could be guarded against to a large extent by certain educational measures. The future, despite its lack of traditional stability, looked good.

The Plowden Committee was not alone in holding this view. The committee appointed by the Education Department of the British Council of Churches to 'enquire into the state and needs of RE' had itself set up a small group to 'assess the implications of the present theological ferment' and this group's report opened with these words:

> To understand the present theological ferment one must place it in its historical context – the context of recent changes in our culture and learning in general. We have come to the end of a culture period dominated by history and archaeology. We have been projected into a period in which, for as long as we can now foresee, we are likely to be dominated by science and technology.[3]

This antithesis between interest in history and interest in science was taken further in a later passage from the same paper:

> The spectacular successes of the scientific method in discovery and demonstration have given it a prestige value which almost automatically serves to down-grade other methods of approach as being of less precision and reliability. The emphasis of the scientific temper upon the continuous discovery of *new* truth tends to play down the value of truth which appears to base its claim upon its antiquity and permanence.[4]

To put it in very crude terms these passages reflect a period in which 'Tomorrow's World' was the sort of quasi-educational programme which would attract TV viewers, and the thought of all those technological goodies which were to come captured people's total attention and interest and made history in particular irrelevant and boring. Science and tech-

120

nology were the new gods who were calling their chosen people towards a promised land flowing with instant milk and deglutinized honey.

Obviously the British Council of Churches group were aware of great dangers in the developing situation, but once again the only dangers identified were spiritual dangers. There were in any case spiritual benefits to be noted as well.

> The enormous expansion of knowledge and the consequent power to control environment have increased man's sense of 'fullness of life' and of responsibility for the use of his powers for the elimination of disease, poverty and suffering.[5]

Again, the future, despite its loss of traditional culture, looked good. There was little sense of 'the heavy swell of an unknown sea' or 'inevitable birth pangs' in these passages I have quoted. In *Religion and the Secondary School* I 'fully endorsed' all that the group had said, and I chose the Teilhard quotations for the end of the book not because they injected a corrective note of impending danger, but because they indicated the continuing need for *faith* even in an age dominated by scientific discovery and technological advance:

> Without the taste for life mankind, even under the spur of immediate fear or desire, would soon cease from work it knew to be doomed in advance. And stricken at the very source of the impetus which sustains it, it would disintegrate from nausea or revolt and crumble into dust.[6]

Those words strike home today with appalling relevance. Our worshippers at the altar of 'Tomorrow's World' have either become ardent disciples of the new reforming prophet, the environmentalist documentary, or else, having turned their backs on the future in total disillusionment, have been finding distraction in the lives of our various Tudor monarchs, or even in the growth of Victorian imperial splendour. The past is now all-absorbing. Science is dethroned and the future has become boring in its frightfulness.

Again I have been employing very crude terms in which to

identify the prevailing mood. But the crude terms do reflect a real crisis, such as was foreseen by Teilhard, possibly a crisis in which the waves of the unknown sea will overwhelm us even before we have got out of sight of land. Can one preserve 'the taste for life' in the face of predictions such as the following?

> Western society is in the process of completing the rape and murder of the planet for economic gain. And, sadly, most of the rest of the world is eager for the opportunity to emulate our behaviour. But the underdeveloped peoples will be denied that opportunity – the days of plunder are drawing inexorably to a close. Most of the people who are going to die in the greatest cataclysm in the history of man have already been born.[7]

Teilhard claimed that in our reaction to the world (to its very existence and to its future development) 'there is no middle way between the two alternatives of absolute optimism or absolute pessimism'. Can there be any optimism at all in the face of current environmentalist predictions? Can anyone really offer 'in support of hope', to use Teilhard's phrase, 'rational invitations to an act of faith'?[8]

Certainly all kinds of invitations to faith are being eagerly accepted on all sides at the moment. Some drug-cults appear to be entirely pessimistic and escapist, but others are offering access to 'reality' in the face of the disintegration of the 'unreal' world of technological society. Similarly much of the support offered by astrology in its various booming developments is of a pessimistic, fatalistic kind, and yet many of its adherents claim that it can give not only that inner assurance that enables one to tackle the many tasks that face the world, but also the guidance necessary for tackling them successfully.

What of Christianity? Are the invitations to faith which *it* offers either persuasive or rational enough to continue to claim precedence within our western civilization? This is obviously not a question to be embarked on at all seriously at this distance from the back cover, but a totally relevant point does need to be made. The effect of Christianity has been a somewhat ambivalent one. On the one hand there is some justice in the charge that the Judaeo-Christian tradition, with its anthropocentric creation myths, is in large measure responsible (even if not deliberately so) for the western world's feeling that 'no item in the physical creation had any purpose save to serve man's purposes'. In every continent except Asia (and possibly, at one remove, there as well) 'by destroying pagan animism, Christianity made it possible to exploit nature in a mood of indifference to natural objects'.[9]

On the other hand the following passage is not so untypical of Christian writing as some would have us believe:

> The Christian tradition of Western Europe, and consequently also of the Western World, rests on certain postulates which are indispensable but are often ignored. The first is the essential unity of the whole created order – or, if you like, of nature, including human nature. Man may be more than a part of nature, but he is that. At every turn he is dependent on his natural environment, and if he is to prosper in the long run it must be as a partner with nature in the production and utilization of its resources, not as its lord exploiting nature for his own ends; that way leads to sterilization and death.

That passage was not (as one might have expected) written by the Bishop of Kingston in 1972, but by the Archbishop of Canterbury in 1944.[10] It is obvious, however, that this is the message which *every* Christian leader throughout the world should be stressing at the present time, and one which needs working out in very practical terms by every single practising Christian, however widely or narrowly his responsibilities may extend.

The urgency of this whole issue lies in the fact that the decisions we take in the next few years are the ones which *may* enable there to be a future after all, or which will merely hasten the days of 'sterilization and death'. Clearly this

123

doctrine of 'the essential unity of the whole created order' is one which must figure predominantly in any presentation of Christian belief in the RE classroom, and one which must be 'commended' by the activities and expressed-attitudes of the schools, both church and county.

But the situation is one which may well call not only for possible changes of emphasis in the *content* of the Christian faith as expressed in an educational context. If it appears that we have in fact already passed the point at which effective decision-making could have occurred, and that the ecological cataclysm is now inevitable and at the most only to be held off for a few decades, then obviously the whole educational *strategy* of the church may have to alter in the face of such a crisis.

Questions like this have been ignored in the body of this book. The first five, staid chapters were written with the assumption that life is going on much as before, only perhaps better. They were written this way because educationists have been thinking this way throughout the period I have been examining and commenting on. Let us only hope that those who actually hold power in the world are by now sufficiently alerted to be prepared to initiate the massive steps needed to avert the cataclysm. But in the midst of that hope let us bear in mind some words from that ostensibly out-of-date document, entitled *Religious Teaching for Schools*, the Cambridgeshire Agreed Syllabus:

> Religious faith is always exposed to the temptation to acquiesce in things as they are, or to let history take its course, on the ground that the Lord of history knows what he is doing and will in his own time bring the world into conformity with his purpose. But the God of Christian faith is a God who will have men to be his 'fellow-workers'. It is God that 'worketh in us both to will and to do': yet for that very reason we are to 'work out our own salvation'.[11]

I wish you good working.

NOTES

1. Published by the SCM Press in 1968.

2. P. Teilhard de Chardin, *The Phenomenon of Man*, Collins 1959, p. 214.

3. *Religion and the Secondary School*, pp. 153f.

4. *Ibid.*, p. 156.

5. *Ibid.*, p. 159.

6. *The Phenomenon of Man*, p. 232.

7. Paul R. Ehrlich, in *Ramparts*, September 1969.

8. *The Phenomenon of Man*, p. 234.

9. Lynn White Jr, in *Science*, vol. 155, March 1967.

10 William Temple, *The Church Looks Forward*, Macmillan 1944, p. 79.

11. CUP 1949, p. 9.

For Further Reading

Obviously the various reports (see below) which have been referred to and quoted from will repay direct study. So will the other books whose details are given in the notes to each chapter. *In addition* to these I would mention (chapter by chapter):

Chapter 2

R. S. Peters (ed.), *Perspectives on Plowden*, Routledge & Kegan Paul 1967.

Chapter 3

Prospects and Problems for Religious Education, HMSO 1971.

J. W. D. Smith, *Religious Education in a Secular Setting*, SCM Press 1969.

K. Gibberd, *Teaching Religion in Schools*, Longmans 1970.

D. W. Gundry, *The Teacher and World Religions*, James Clarke 1968.

J. R. Hinnells (ed.), *Comparative Religion in Education*, Oriel Press 1970.

G. Parrinder (ed.), *Teaching about Religions*, Harrap 1971.

Chapters 4 and 5

F. H. Hilliard *et al.*, *Christianity in Education*, Allen & Unwin 1963.

N. Smart, *The Teacher and Christian Belief*, James Clarke 1966.

K. Bliss *et al.*, *Education and the Nature of Man*, WCC 1967.

G. Heawood, *The Humanist/Christian Frontier*, SPCK 1968.

M. V. C. Jeffreys, *Truth is not Neutral*, Religious Education Press 1969.

C. M. Jones, *Worship in the Secondary School*, Religious Education Press 1969.

Chapter 6
H. Montefiore, *Can Man Survive?*, Collins Fontana Books 1970.

The main reports referred to are:

Half our Future, HMSO 1963 (Newsom Report)
Children and their Primary Schools, HMSO 1967 (Plowden Report)
Primary Education in Wales, HMSO 1967 (Gittins Report)
The Fourth R, National Society/SPCK 1970 (Durham Report)
Religion in Secondary Schools, Evans/Methuen 1971 (Schools Council Working Paper 36)
Partners in Education, National Society/SPCK 1971 (Carlisle Report)

See also the later Schools Council Working Paper on *Religious Education in the Primary School*, Evans/Methuen 1972.